REBELS
WITH A
CAUSE

Helen Garvy

**A collective memoir of the hopes,
rebellions and repression of the 1960s**

Shire Press

typography and production by Dickie Magidoff
cover adapted from film poster designed by Kevin Gaor,
with photo from Robert Joyce Photography Collection,
Courtesy of Historical Collections and Labor Archives,
Special Collections Library, The Pennsylvania State University

Library of Congress Control Number: 20079240422
ISBN13#: 978-0-918828-22-4

Shire Press
644 Hester Creek Road
Los Gatos, CA 95033
(408) 353-4253
www.ShirePressandFilms.com

Contents

Preface

> It isn't the rebels that cause the troubles of the world, it's the troubles that cause the rebels.
>
> *Carl Oglesby, president of SDS, 1965-66*

The Sixties began sleepily on the heels of a decade of modest prosperity combined with significant areas of poverty. Pride in the American ideals of freedom, justice, and equality conflicted with much of what we saw around us — legal and *de facto* segregation, the ever-present atomic bomb, the Cold War, and HUAC and Senator Joseph McCarthy's intimidating witch-hunts. It was an era of conformity and contradictions. Things were quiet on the surface, but all was not well.

The tone changed after 1960 and the decade was anything but quiet. It was a time of social change, war, and repression that woke up the country and that still affects both members of that generation and the country as a whole to this day. The victories of that decade changed the country profoundly; the scars from that decade are still raw.

SDS

> SDS stood as the catalyst, vanguard, and personification of that decade of defiance. *Kirkpatrick Sale, SDS*

Students for a Democratic Society is remembered today primarily as the spearhead of the opposition to the war in Vietnam, beginning with the 1965 March on Washington and ending with the Weathermen — but it was far more that that. SDS was a uniquely American movement that grew and evolved in response to the times. It was an organization that spanned ten years, with eventually over 400 chapters in almost all fifty states. It encompassed a wide variety of issues during a very turbulent decade. And it was the largest and most active student organization of its time.

SDS began in 1960 with a handful of members and high ideals, inspired by the civil rights movement and initially concerned with equality, peace, economic justice, university reform, and 'participatory democracy.' America was just beginning to face the injustices of segregation and racism. Those injustices outraged us, and slowly a movement for change began to grow on the campuses.

Then came a war in Vietnam at a time when few had even heard of that far-off land. SDS grew rapidly as the war expanded relentlessly, and our polite protests turned into stronger and more determined resistance — and increasing frustration and rage. By 1969, SDS had been transformed into a hard-hitting protest movement against the war in Vietnam, with over 100,000 members and chapters all across the country at large universities, public and private colleges, and even high schools. Mixed in with all this, although we didn't understand it at the time, was a concerted government effort, spearheaded by the FBI, to destroy SDS and other parts of the movement.

Two years later, for a variety of reasons that I'll explore later, SDS no longer existed as a national organization, although its members continued on — and its impact is still felt today.

Many of the ideas fought for by SDS throughout a decade of social upheaval are now integrated into American society. Many of today's movements for a better society can trace their roots back to the Sixties — including a plethora of local groups and alternative educational, cultural, and political institutions. The women's movement, the environmental movement, and support for third world struggles in the US and progressive movements around the world are all a legacy of the times that shaped — and were shaped by — SDS and the movements for social change of the 1960s.

Although those who journeyed with SDS for part or all of that decade have grown and changed in the years that followed, most who were active in SDS still hold the same values today and are still actively trying to make the world a better place.

THE FILM

In late 1998 and early 1999 — long before George W. Bush's war in Iraq — I filmed interviews with more than two dozen SDS activists and edited those into a feature documentary film, *Rebels With A Cause*, which was released in 2000.

My goal was to capture that period as it was for those who came of age in the Sixties and became involved in SDS and the protests of that time. I wanted to give a sense of who we were, as well as preserve and pass on some pieces of history. I also wanted to show not just what we did but why we did it.

What SDS was about, more than anything, was building a movement for social change and getting people to join with us — not just to join SDS but to join our cause: to end discrimination and injustice, to end poverty, to end the war. The formation and growth of a movement is a mysterious thing. Some comes from the times and some from luck — but much also comes 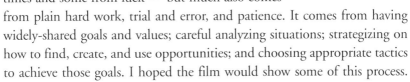 from plain hard work, trial and error, and patience. It comes from having widely-shared goals and values; careful analyzing situations; strategizing on how to find, create, and use opportunities; and choosing appropriate tactics to achieve those goals. I hoped the film would show some of this process.

I especially wanted to show the trajectory of the decade — the changes in SDS, and in individuals. I also wanted to go beyond the flashy and well-known events to explore some of the subtleties, the underpinnings, and the unnoticed or overlooked issues and actions of those times. I wanted to put faces on the actors, to help the audience understand what drew different kinds of people to SDS and what it was we cared about so deeply. I wanted those involved to tell the story directly — and to tell it from the grass-roots level. Many of the activists interviewed went on to become leaders at the regional and national levels — but they all began in local groups and it's largely those activities I focused on.

I filmed people individually, at different times in different cities. I then edited the interviews together to create a conversation about some of the events and ideas of that decade.

Some of the people I interviewed were — and still are — good friends; others didn't know each other. That's in part due to the nature of SDS, which was both in some sense family but also spanned ten years and a very large country so that people who were very active in one period often didn't know those active in another period. A 'generation' in a student organization is very short.

In selecting people to interview, I tried to choose people who were representative of an SDS that varied with time, place, and personalities, as well as politics. I usually sought more than one person for each part of the story in order to be able to create a dialogue.

I was not an impartial outside observer. I was a part of that generation and was very involved in SDS and many of its activities. My thoughts were influenced by those experiences and also by several SDS reunions we've had in the intervening years. As I began the film project, I was also guided by conversations with and letters from over two hundred former SDS members who shared their ideas of what they thought was important to say.

We learned a tremendous amount during the Sixties. At our best, we were able to learn from our experiences and our successes and failures as we went along. At our worst, we weren't. I hope sharing some of those ideas and experiences might be of use to future generations.

THE BOOK

The idea for the book began when I realized I had a lot of material from the original interviews that didn't fit into the film but was both interesting and historically valuable. Expanding the film into a book allowed me to cover some areas in more depth than I was able to in the film and also allowed me to explore new areas.

This is a collective memoir — a quilt, a mosaic.

We were a group of people who shared many similarities but who also came from different backgrounds, with different experiences before and during the Sixties. Those experiences and backgrounds shaped us and made for both differences amongst us and also a stronger whole that really was more than the sum of its parts. What we shared usually overshadowed our differences.

This book doesn't present an unbroken continuous linear history and isn't meant as a comprehensive history. Some events and thoughts are given more time than others; many things are left out. That was due to both the interview material I had to work with and an attempt to cover so much territory in a single book.

I wrote this book both for those who know nothing of the Sixties, or only a few vague and probably incorrect stereotypes, as well as for those who were participants in some part, or parts, of the story. And all those in between.

I hope you will enjoy the individual pieces of the quilt and also come away with a picture of the whole. The movement grew, like a quilt, one piece at a time.

I chose a conversational format for the film — and kept it for the book — because that was an important part of who we were. We shared our experiences, our perspectives, our views on what was happening around us and what we should do in response. Sometimes we agreed, sometimes we didn't. I tried to create a whole story, a conversation, while also letting you see who the individual speakers were, as if you were in the room. Sometimes the conversation, like all conversations, is a little choppy. Some parts will likely be of greater interest to some people than others.

I have used first names only in the text to lessen clutter — and also because who the speakers are both matters and doesn't. Their stories and memories are individual — but they are also representative of so many others. For a short cast of characters, see page vii. For a little more detail on the interviewees, see page 245. For basic information on SDS's organizational structure, see page 252.

In editing the book, I tried to stay close to the original interviews and to keep their informal conversational quality, editing only when necessary to allow spoken words to read a little more easily. I made some changes to maintain the flow or eliminate mis-starts or digressions. I generally omitted ellipses and brackets to facilitate reading but always tried to remain true to the original interviews and the speakers. If you want to hear and see the speakers, check out the film (see order form on last page).

I have tried not to get in the way of the speakers, to let them tell the story as much as possible, adding only occasional comments for background.

Although SDS was the largest organization of the 1960s, it didn't stand alone. It was part of what we simply called 'the movement'. Speakers often use the term 'we' loosely to mean SDS or a broader group they were working with or the movement in general.

Told through the eyes of SDS members, this story is about far more than SDS. It's about the values, motivations, and actions of a generation that lost its innocence but gained a sense of power and purpose. It's about young people who questioned and challenged their government on issues of basic values and policies. It's about a decade that changed America.

Cast of Characters

(for more information on interviewees, see page 245)

Alan Haber. University of Michigan; SDS president, 1960–62

Alice Embree. University of Texas; *RAT,* New York

Bernardine Dohrn. University of Chicago Law School; inter-organizational secretary, 1967–68; Weatherman

Bill Ayers. University of Michigan; regional organizer, 1968–69; inter-organizational secretary, 1969–70; Weatherman

Bob Ross. University of Michigan, University of Chicago

Carl Davidson. Penn State; U of Nebraska; vice president, 1966–67; inter-organizational secretary, 1967–68

Carl Oglesby. SDS president, 1965–66

Carol Glassman. Smith College, Newark ERAP project

Carolyn Craven. Goucher College; national office staff, 1964-65; San Francisco regional office, 1965–67

Casey Hayden. SNCC staff, Chicago ERAP project

Cathy Wilkerson. Swarthmore College; national staff, 1965–66; Washington regional office, 1967–68; Weatherman

Dick Flacks. University of Michigan, U of Chicago, UC Santa Barbara

Elizabeth Stanley. Harvard

Jane Adams. Southern Illinois University; Iowa-Midwest regional organizer, 1965; national secretary, 1966

Jeff Shero(Nightbyrd). U of Texas; vice president, 1965–66; editor of *RAT,* New York

Juan Gonzalez. Columbia

Judy Schiffer Perez. University of Texas; Los Angeles region

Junius Williams. Amherst College, Newark ERAP project, Yale Law

Marilyn Salzman Webb. Chicago, Washington

Mark Kleiman. Los Angeles; Chicago, high school and draft organizer; San Francisco regional office

Mike Spiegel. Harvard; national secretary, 1967–68

Robert Pardun. University of Texas; education secretary, 1967–68

Sharon Jeffrey Lehrer. University of Michigan, Cleveland ERAP

Steve Max. New York; field secretary 1962–63; director of SDS's Political Education Project, 1964–65

Sue Eanet Klonsky. Cornell chapter; NY and LA regional offices; national staff

Todd Gitlin. Harvard; SDS president, 1963–64; coordinator of SDS's Peace Research & Education Project, 1964–65

Tom Hayden. U of Michigan; SDS president, 1962–63; Newark ERAP

Vivian Leburg Rothstein. Berkeley, Chicago ERAP project

1
Setting the Scene

When we were kids the United States was the wealthiest and strongest country in the world; the only nation with the atom bomb, the least scarred by modern war, an initiator of the United Nations that we thought would distribute Western influence throughout the world. Freedom and equality for each individual; government of, by, and for the people — these American values we found good, principles by which we could live as men. Many of us began maturing in complacency.   *SDS Port Huron Statement, 1962*

On the television was the image of fire-hoses being turned on people, spraying them across the street. They were being thrown every which way by these fire-hoses. And the commentator was saying that the reason this was happening was that these people wanted to vote. And I can remember turning to my father and saying, "What does this mean? What are they talking about, the right to vote? They don't vote? Why can't they vote?"   *Mike*

You've got to remember that in those days the South was segregated. Maryland was a secessionist state. I was at an all-white women's college just outside Baltimore. I couldn't eat in most of the restaurants in Baltimore, I couldn't try on clothes in the stores. I used to have to go into a store, buy everything I thought I wanted, bring it back to my dorm room, try it on, and then return what didn't fit and what I didn't want because I couldn't go into the dressing rooms in the stores. Goucher College owned property where there was a shopping center but I could not eat at the snack counter there. I had to sit in the balcony at movie theaters.   *Carolyn*

Port Arthur was a racist town. I remember vividly, when I was in high school, going to the public library — and blacks were not allowed. There were black bathrooms and white bathrooms, there were black water fountains and white water fountains.

Judy

In Carbondale, I was in the band and our band was an integrated group, three or four black players in it. We took a trip to the local roller rink, which was in a little town 6–7 miles away, and they wouldn't let the black kids in.

Jane

University of Texas dorms were segregated, university sports were segregated, and there were still restaurants that wouldn't serve blacks — and Hispanics.

Alice

I went to the University of North Dakota. The Sioux Indians who had been doing migrant field work, who'd have money in their pockets after harvest season, were not allowed to try on clothing in the department stores, nor were they able to go into the bars and have a beer. So there was Sioux Indian agitation for basic rights. What more racist experience could you have than that people were so dirty that they couldn't try on clothes. So I lasted there a year. Then I went to the University of Texas and the civil rights movement was happening and I got involved.

Jeff

We would be monitored at the University of Michigan if we went out with men of color and if anybody did that, the dean of women would send a letter home to the parents, notifying the parents, and would not write a letter to support that student to get into graduate school.

Sharon

At the age of nine, I went to try out for Little League. Everybody knew I was this really great first baseman, and I came up and they said, "You can't try out because you're a girl."

Marilyn

I remember growing up and having so few things that women could really do.

Alice

We were a generation where abortion was still illegal and when I went to college it was common for women to have illegal abortions, with dangerous consequences. I had several friends who became sterile from illegal abortions. And if you were found out to be pregnant when you were in college, you were automatically expelled.

Cathy

My grandfather was a very strong patriarch and he was very opposed to women going to college.   *Marilyn*

All of us had been forced to wear dresses to school. We were of the generation where our futures had been closely proscribed as small girl children as to what was expected of us and what was allowed. So it was all very new for us to be breaking out and saying we want to define ourselves.   *Cathy*

We were pushing out the walls that said that to be a woman you had to get married. When I went to college, not one woman friend thought about going to law school. Not one thought about medical school. It was not an option for women. We didn't think about it.   *Sharon*

I was one of six women in our law school class. Having so few women was a degrading and humiliating experience. It was a man's world and it was assumed that law was a man's world.   *Bernardine*

I was trying to finish my dissertation for my Ph.D. and — it took me years to incorporate what had happened — I had finished all my coursework and exams and I had to get a committee together to supervise my dissertation. I wanted to do a dissertation on the pre-schools. I soon learned, though, that the only way I could get that committee together was by a *quid pro quo*. I went to each professor I thought would be on it and showed them my work. That's when the *quid pro quo* became obvious — you sleep with me and I'll be on your committee or you don't have a committee. It was not only said that way, but it was very blatant. I was pinned against the wall and aggressively kissed by one professor who asked me to come in and talk about my work. And I had all my papers there and they just fell on the floor. That was really, really shocking to me. And another professor, one I'd thought was my mentor, came over to my apartment and said he wanted to give me a bath. It was more than daunting. I could not get a committee together and never ended up being able to complete my Ph.D. The saddest part is that I did not at the time see that as sexist or as harassment or as political, I saw it as something that was wrong with me.   *Marilyn*

The double standard was firmly in force which said that a women should maintain her virginity at all costs — but men were supposed to hit on women and were supposed to be sexually experienced. And when you have a moral code that says men should be sexually experienced and should be aggressive and should always be trying to get everything they can get and girls are supposed to be virginal and pure, and if they have sex they are practically whores and prostitutes and sluts, you have a major contradiction in the culture.

Jane

College administrators had the most ridiculous and repressive rules on the campuses. I remember one campus where the halls were actually patrolled by guards with dogs. And the guards would listen for sounds of wrong-doing — men in women's rooms or vice-versa. People would be expelled if the dog sniffed you out. At other schools the rule was that three of a couple's four feet had to be on the floor at any given time. It was this kind of silliness. And over and over you met people whose college careers had been ruined because they had been expelled for sex — which then became completely acceptable a couple of years later. In fact a couple of years later the administration was wishing people would engage in sex instead of doing all the other things they were doing, like taking over buildings.

Steve

The local newspaper had job advertisements by gender — men's jobs, women's jobs.

Carol

My mom was a single parent, raising me on a secretary's salary. She got me braces on my teeth, dresses for the prom, and she put me through college. And she did the same for my sister. So I knew from the inside how difficult it was to function in that setting. And my mom talked about that so I grew up with a sense of women's issues.

Casey

> . . . Our comfort was penetrated by events too troubling to dismiss. First, the permeating and victimizing fact of human degradation, symbolized by the Southern struggle against racial bigotry, compelled most of us from silence to activism. Second, the enclosing fact of the Cold War, symbolized by the presence of the Bomb, brought awareness that we ourselves, and our friends, and millions of abstract "others" we knew more directly because of our common peril, might die at any time.   *Port Huron Statement*

I got very involved in competitive speech in high school and won a national original oratory contest with a speech called "Peace or Freedom" advocating the nuclear destruction of the Soviet Union now. So you see, my politics changed.

Carl O

When I entered Penn State as a freshman, the first thing I found out was that ROTC was compulsory. So in addition to my matriculation card and my freshman beanie, I was issued an army uniform and a rifle and was expected to show up three days a week on the drill field. This did not sit well with me, especially for a greaser kid who was into rebellion and James Dean and all that — I did not see myself as somebody marching around in an army uniform, and did not like the idea of the army generally.   *Carl D*

I saw the aftermath of World War II and I'm sure that made a peace activist forever of me. When I was eleven or twelve, my father was advisor on Jewish affairs to the Occupation Army, so we moved to Germany and I saw what the war had left. Coming to the town of Frankfurt and seeing these beautiful buildings just in rubble, and rubble in the street, and crosses planted in the rubble where they haven't even gotten bodies out yet. It just sort of blew me away, the scars of war, without understanding at that point what the issues of the war were. It was something very painful, searing to see.   *Alan*

They issued us dog-tags so that they could figure out who we were from our charred remains. And we had these air raid drills where the siren goes off, you crawl under your desk, you cover up the back of your neck with your hands, you roll into a little ball, and, as more and more of this information comes out about what a nuclear explosion really is, it becomes obvious that you're going to be buried in your school no matter what.   *Robert*

> While these and other problems either directly oppressed us or rankled our consciences and became our own subjective concerns, we began to see complicated and disturbing paradoxes in our surrounding America. The declaration 'all men are created equal . . . ' rang hollow before the facts of Negro life in the South and the big cities of the North. The proclaimed peaceful intentions of the United States contradicted its economic and military investments in the Cold War status quo."   *Port Huron Statement*

Growing up in the 1950s in a place like Aliquippa [Pennsylvania] had a lot of alienation to it. As a teenager, I had always sensed that something wasn't quite right. America, at least what we were taught in school, seemed to offer a lot of promise, but there was an unreality to it that I could never quite put my finger on. When James Dean's movie, *Rebel Without a Cause*, came to town, I went to see it and I was just fascinated. I saw it thirteen times.   *Carl D*

I was raised in the fifties on the rhetoric of democracy and equality and fairness for all — and a reality that clearly was not that.   *Cathy*

For me, growing up in the Midwest and starting to look at the broader world was a jarring conflict with what I'd been taught because I believed — I absolutely believed — in the Pledge of Allegiance and the Constitution and the notion that we were good, and better, and best.   *Bernardine*

I think it's a part of the soul that people want to serve, to make things better, to have their dreams come true.   *Alan*

Some would have us believe that Americans feel contentment amidst prosperity — but might it not better be called a glaze above deeply-felt anxieties about their role in the new world? And if these anxieties produce a developed indifference to human affairs, do they not as well produce a yearning to believe there *is* an alternative to the present, that something *can* be done to change the circumstances in the school, the workplaces, the bureaucracies, the government? It is to this latter yearning, at once the spark and engine of change, that we direct our present appeal.

Port Huron Statement

2
SDS Begins

> We are people of this generation . . . looking uncomfortably to a world we inherit. *SDS's Port Huron Statement*

Although originally established in 1905 by Upton Sinclair, Jack London, Clarence Darrow and others as the Intercollegiate Socialist Society, for all practical purposes SDS began in 1960 after it was reorganized and re-energized following a period of relative inactivity, took the name Students for a Democratic Society, and elected Alan Haber as its first president.

At its peak in the late 1960s, SDS had over 100,000 members, 400 chapters on campuses all over the country, and was the largest student organization of the decade. But in 1960 there were just a few dozen members, mostly centered around the University of Michigan.

HUMAN RIGHTS IN THE NORTH

In the fall of 1959, I kept looking for other people who were like me, who cared about things, and I saw this poster announcing a meeting and it said: Come to a meeting to organize a conference on Human Rights in the North. I thought: I'll try this, I've tried other things, I didn't have a lot of hope. I went to this meeting, there were a half dozen to a dozen people there, and there was this man called Al Haber up in front. And he started talking about this conference on Human Rights in the North. And he was talking about civil rights and race relations and black & white and stuff like that. And all of a sudden here was a man who had a vision, who obviously had passion and cared, and had a sense of organizing, of what it took to get people to come together to do something.   *Sharon*

The conference on Human Rights in the North was an act of brilliance by Al Haber. He saw that the issue of racism in the North, and discrimination, could be the basis of a student movement. The crazy thing about this is that he figured this out before the sit-in movement began.   *Bob*

Sharon Jeffrey

This was considered a pretty radical idea because most people had no idea that there was a problem in the North around segregation and discrimination and civil rights. This was prior to the civil rights movement, this was prior to any sit-ins, and so it was a fairly innovative idea. And in the midst of talking about that he also talked about the creation of a national student movement and that he wanted to invite students from other campuses to join with us in this conference. I was very excited.

Then February 1st, 1960, four black students from Greensboro, North Carolina, sat down at a lunch counter in Woolworth's and asked for a cup of coffee. They weren't served — and they were arrested. And that was the beginning of this whole civil rights sit-in movement that spread across the South.   *Sharon*

It was obvious when the sit-ins happened, that our perspective changed, that we wanted to be part of this larger national activism.   *Alan*

We invited them to our conference in the spring of 1960.   *Sharon*

A lot of SNCC [Student Nonviolent Coordinating Committee] people did come — it was part of a solidarity that was becoming established. *Alan*

They galvanized that conference because here were real students doing something. And it set off sympathetic picket lines all across the northern campuses. At the University of Michigan, every Saturday for two hours, we had picket lines for the dime stores that were the same as the ones in the South. *Sharon*

It was a momentous day. I was all of 16½ at the time. I was very nervous. I'd never been in a demonstration or a march or a picket line and I was apprehensive. We all dressed up for demonstrations in those days. I put on my only tweed jacket and a tie and I walked on this picket line. And that broke the crust of apathy from myself and hundreds of others and it changed my whole trajectory in life. *Bob*

Alan Haber

This became an opportunity to talk to students on campus about the issues in the world — in this case it was the civil rights issue. And it provided an opportunity to organize and recruit and bring people into other issues that were related to this issue. It was a very exciting time, a very vibrant time.

I was the kind of person who'd talk about these issues to anyone at any time. Back then we all had a common bathroom in the dormitory, so we'd all be in front of the sinks together, we'd all be in the showers together — and what a great opportunity to be able to talk to people. I had an audience. And that was the place I did most of my organizing and most of my recruiting. Then these student would come to the picket lines — and then they would have an experience and would talk to their friends and they'd bring their friends. *Sharon*

PORT HURON

The next big event in the formation of SDS was the decision to write a document that would help define the organization.

There were a lot of students who had responded to the civil rights movement but the North wasn't as segregated, so to just have a national support group for the South seemed essential but not enough. And there were these other issues — the campus paternalism, the bomb, the arms race. So there was a lot of thinking about how can we best form an organization. We brought together 50-100 people to an Ann Arbor retreat in the dead of winter in 1961. And the conclusion was that we had to have a vision first.   *Tom*

For its 1962 convention, held at a labor union camp in Port Huron, Michigan, SDS members decided to write a document that would reflect how they saw the world and what they were all about — a manifesto of sorts. It began that spring with letters among members, then a draft document was written by Tom Hayden, debated over several days at the convention, and issued as the Port Huron Statement.

FDR-CIO Camp,
Port Huron, Michigan

There was something that connected us, we knew that, and it would be useful to try and express it. We decided to do a manifesto for the convention.   *Alan*

Someone said we need an explicit articulation of our goals and values and strategies.   *Bob*

Bob Ross and Tom Hayden, SDS convention, 1968

The process that was decided on was to ask everybody in the organization what should be in a manifesto, so we put out a series of newsletters asking that question. What is important to you, what facts or values or information should be in a statement that we would make. And people wrote back letters and we edited and pulled out pithy paragraphs that we strung together into a newsletter that was then sent back to the membership. And that was then to be pulled together into a draft text.   *Alan*

The meeting concluded that I would go draft this vision and we would then mimeograph it and circulate it.   *Tom*

Port Huron was to be the place where all the bits and pieces were to be woven together and then discussed.   *Alan*

When we got to the convention we took the document that he wrote and broke it down into sections and then we would meet in little groups so that everybody had the opportunity to debate and discuss it in small group settings prior to the large debate session.   *Sharon*

And it was just sitting around in small groups, talking about your values and how they applied to politics. Suddenly something that should have been 10–20 pages became 40–50 pages. It became the document that all the people who met at this Port Huron meeting could weigh, and divide up, and transform, and take ownership of, and re-write. And that became the Port Huron Statement.   *Tom*

THE

PORT HURON STATEMENT

. . . we seek the establishment of a democracy of individual participation governed by two central aims: that the individual share in those social decisions determining the quality and direction of his life; that society be organized to encourage independence in men and provide the media for their common participation . . .

Students for a Democratic Society

My major memory of Port Huron is sleep deprivation. We were in sessions 18 hours a day working on this. We had the exuberance and energy of people who didn't know anything couldn't be done.

We have a Yiddish word 'chutzpah.' The assumption that this group of 20-year old people could change the country and issue a statement that people would be interested in, that alone was, as we say, 'chutzpadik.' But that was itself exciting, that people thought they meant something in the world.   *Dick*

Dick Flacks, 1964

And the key theme there was 'participatory democracy' — and this was something that somehow had a resonance to it, it had a sing-song to it, it just sort of resonated within everybody. And everybody went: whew, this is really significant, because it touched very deeply the soul of who we were.

Sharon

One phrase that a university professor in Ann Arbor, Arnold Kaufman, kept referring to — participatory democracy — struck me as a good phrase to describe what we were trying to accomplish and how we were trying to accomplish it. We wanted to have a fully democratic society and the way to achieve it was through the democratic process by activism. So the means and the end were kind of parallel.

What we, the activists, were about was the resurrection of the decentralized democracy or the direct democracy or the town-meeting democracy — there was a kind of element in America of history from the bottom up.

Tom

The vision of participatory democracy is that people, separately and together, have the power to direct the key institutions of the society, power to control their own lives.   *Bob*

It seemed to touch us because it had two parts to it. One was: it was a vision — that we could have a vision of a society that was a participatory democratic society. And at the same time it represented a means to get there — that is: we could do this, right now, ourselves, with each other, in this political group, together. So it had both the long-term visionary aspect to it as well as: this is something we can do right now. So it represented a very significant value — that we really cared about individuals in the society participating in the decisions that affect them. So it was the cornerstone of SDS, and, I think, what was its major contribution.   *Sharon*

Democracy was something that you go out and do every day. It wasn't merely voting for representatives every couple of years, but that you found ways of implementing democracy every time you got up in the morning. You didn't wait for the government to pass a civil rights law if you couldn't get into the barber shop, you opened the doors and you went in. I mean, that was the essence of what participatory democracy was about.   *Steve*

We also thought that the economy should be democratized — that millionaires shouldn't get millions of votes to our one. It meant democratic control of our collective life.   *Bob*

> . . . work should involve incentives worthier than money or survival. It should be educative, not stultifying; creative, not mechanical; self-directed, not manipulated; encouraging independence, a respect for others, a sense of dignity, and a willingness to accept social responsibility . . .   *Port Huron Statement*

And the second major contribution, which was very significant and very important to all of us, was the values section.   *Sharon*

We decided that we should not start with all the problems that everybody knows so well — let's start with what unifies us.   *Alan*

> Human relationships should involve fraternity and honesty.
> We find violence to be abhorrent.
> We regard men as infinitely precious and possessed of unfulfilled capacities for reason, freedom, and love.   *Port Huron Statement*

When we wrote the Port Huron Statement, we used the word 'man' and none of us questioned it. Today, we all question it; today it wouldn't be written that way. When I read that statement now, I cannot read it without saying 'men and women.'   *Sharon*

Steve Max, 1965

The idea that you made your own values, as a group, was a new thing. That values weren't just inherited — and weren't just transmitted from the older generation — but that people could actually sit down and work out an ethical framework, as an organization, and then go and try to live that way, that was not something that was popularly in the culture.   *Steve*

> Making values explicit — an initial task in establishing alternatives — is an activity that has been devalued and corrupted . . . . The questions we might want raised — what is really important? can we live in a different and better way? if we wanted to change society, how would we do it? — are not thought to be questions of a "fruitful, empirical nature," and thus are brushed aside.   *Port Huron Statement*

Port Huron meeting hall

What was astounding was that when we walked out of the building there was the most gorgeous display of the northern lights, the *aurora borealis*. Now I was never much for signs from heaven, this was as close as I've probably come and I don't even think it was one. But nonetheless there we were, having completed this great labor, been up all night, the *aurora borealis*, dawn coming up, and you really did have the feeling that something new and dramatic had started there.   *Steve*

Port Huron was a real born-again kind of experience in today's terms. People really had a transformative experience. It could have been the intoxication that comes with no sleep, it could have been that the sun was always coming up on Lake Huron.

It was a spiritual awakening, as if a spirit inhabited our generation and enabled us to do the things that a previous generation should have done or could have done. There was this feeling that in doing this you were creating some kind of bonds that would last. And that you were actually launching or giving birth to something that would have a lot of energy. People went away changed. It was an organization formed around a spirit or a feeling, it wasn't an organization in the bureaucratic sense.   *Tom*

> The search for truly democratic alternatives to the present, and a commitment to social experimentation with them, is a worthy and fulfilling human enterprise, one which moves us and, we hope, others today. On such a basis do we offer this document of our convictions and analysis: as an effort in understanding and changing the conditions of humanity in the late twentieth century, an effort rooted in the ancient, still unfulfilled conception of man attaining determining influence over his circumstances of life.
>
> *Port Huron Statement*

It was very moving that we had accomplished a self-definition that was useful to others. There were only less than four dozen people at this meeting that is now sort of mythic, there must have been thousands. Well, in some ways there were because that message went back to campuses.   *Alan*

> As students for a democratic society, we are committed to stimulating this kind of social movement, this kind of vision and program in campus and community across the country.   *Port Huron Statement*

3
Early Years

In the summer of 1963 SDS had maybe 1000 members, about twenty chapters, maybe half of which were real. It consisted more of civil rights activists than people coming from anyplace else. It didn't do much, had an aura, produced zillions of documents, was thoughtful, talky. And that's already more than I knew when I became president of the organization.

Todd

But word about SDS was spreading, even to Texas.

I had never heard of SDS, so I read the Port Huron Statement from beginning to end.

Robert

Judy Schiffer and Robert Pardun, Austin, 1964

We were really looking for something and SDS provided a different perspective, a larger perspective.   *Judy*

The important thing about SDS was that it wasn't just a civil rights organization or an anti-war organization, it was a multi-issue organization. One of our slogans at the time was that all of the issues were interconnected.

                                                              Robert

In 1964 I went to this national SDS convention in Pine Hill, NY, and it was an eye-opening, awakening, deep, and profound experience because these people I met were the most insightful, caring, and passionate. And I went back to Texas and said we should just have the biggest SDS chapter in the country.

We got together and by darned if we didn't sit there in front of registration. It was so archaic that people registered by hand, which gave us plenty of time to talk to people coming in and out of registration.   *Jeff*

Jeff Shero, Gary Thiher, Judy Schiffer at registration, Austin, 1964

There was a little card table and there were these energetic people. This is the first time I remember finding out about the organization. Conversations were lively. Issues were related to each other, it wasn't like a single-issue organization, just interested in peace or just interested in civil rights. That had such an impact on me. Suddenly someone was saying these things are connected together, these things don't exist in isolation. People would have conversations late into the night. We'd have meetings and they'd go on for three hours. The conversations would just grow, they'd just mushroom. It was exciting.

Alice

Alice Embree, 1965. Carol McEldowney and Paul Potter in back

We had an SDS chapter coming out of there of about 50-60 and by the end of a whole series of actions on the campus we had a couple of hundred.

Jeff

The real life of SDS was in the chapters, where activities often focused on peace issues, campus issues around everything from dorm rules to free speech — and civil rights.

CIVIL RIGHTS

From the beginning in 1960, SDS built strong connections with the civil rights movement, especially with SNCC, the Student Non-violent Coordinating Committee, the group that came out of the sit-ins.

I went to the founding meeting of SNCC, the Student Nonviolent Coordinating Committee, in the middle of April in 1960, so I again met a lot of the activists from the South.   *Alan*

The people around SDS were the core of student support for SNCC.
                                                                    Casey

I was a rather crusading, idealistic, but non-political editor of the paper when the sit-ins started in the South. I wanted to go south. So Alan sent me, at $60 a week I think it was, to the South, to write pamphlets and report back, to try to activate students in the North.   *Tom*

He wrote about his time in the South and through that many people got a first-hand view inside of what was happening in the South.   *Casey*

Casey Hayden, 1964

I didn't really realize the depth to which the South was still another country. We followed a march of high school students [in McComb, Mississippi] who were marching from their high school across the tracks to break the segregation line in the town. And I'm writing madly and taking notes and sitting at the wheel and all of a sudden the doors are ripped open and Paul [Potter] disappears. It's something like if you're in white-water in a raft and somebody's gone over the side. You have no idea what happened, it takes your mind seconds to process it, but there couldn't be too many explanations because we weren't moving and he was gone. And before I could figure out what had happened, the door on my side of the car was ripped open and I was dragged out.

Both of us were beat up and kicked around by some little mob of guys. When they were done, this photographer who had come out of nowhere said, under his breath, "Get out of town, you're going to be killed tonight."

Tom

I organized a food drive when some sharecroppers had gone on strike from a plantation in Tennessee. We took a carload of food down.

The sheriff came after us at night and I remember my legs collapsed. I had never known that you could get so afraid that your legs would give out. And I was trying to imagine if this happened to me in one night, what it would be like to live every night in the rural areas of the South. We went into town, Fayette, and we were trying to call the Justice Department and yell about the sheriff and all of a sudden there was this mob at the door with chains and clubs and the people we were with said, "You have to leave town now." It wasn't clear what the alternative was but we got in the car and we drove like 110 miles an hour straight out of town, watching in the mirror as these people tried to overtake us. That had a searing effect.   *Tom*

SDS chapters also participated in local civil rights activities.

We went downtown to the Picadilly Restaurant [in Austin] and we started walking back and forth in front of the door. I'd never been on a picket line before. There was a ring of policemen around us. On the other side of the street were people yelling at us. We were seriously outnumbered.

We were being called 'communist' and also 'nigger-lover' — because if you were a white person supporting blacks, that was almost worse than if you were a black person because you were a traitor.   *Robert*

Route 40 used to be the only highway between Washington DC and New York. All of the restaurants along that highway were segregated, blacks could not eat in them. We could not eat in them at all or we could sometimes go to the back door and get food given to us out the back door. And that was all the way to the New Jersey border. So the Route 40 sit-ins were primarily a bunch of college students — we were from Goucher/Johns Hopkins, Morgan State, and Howard — and we got together every Saturday morning and we would divide up and we would picket the restaurants along Route 40. It was scary. It was the first time I ever went to jail; it was the first time I'd ever been around people yelling horrible things at me.   *Carolyn*

Our Friends of SNCC group [at Penn State] always put up literature tables in the student union building. I loved the literature tables, I loved to sit behind them and get into conversations with people. A bunch of people usually came by; one in particular was a stone racist and I loved to debate with him. I'd try to get him to stand there for as long as I could because everybody would start gathering around and we'd be going back and forth. People would listen to me and they'd listen to him — and they'd walk over and open up their wallets and make donations to what we were doing.   *Carl D*

The University of Texas dormitories were segregated. At the end of the year we put out a press release and we leafleted around saying that when President Lyndon Johnson came to Austin to give the commencement address, there would be a demonstration — because his daughter lived in a segregated dorm. Between the time we made up that press release and the time he showed up for commencement, the dorms were integrated!   *Robert*

There was a protest against segregated schools in Chester, Pennsylvania, which was the town next door to Swarthmore. This was the fall of 1963. The parents were striking against the overcrowding of the black school, they had terrible housing conditions and slum landlords, all of the roads were not yet paved, they didn't have regular garbage collection, they didn't have street lights or stop signs.

The schools were segregated because the way the zoning worked was that they zoned all the black kids into one school and all the white neighborhoods were in other schools. The black school was far more overcrowded and had less supplies. It was really overt segregation even though it wasn't legal segregation the way it was in the South. It was *de facto* and obvious, blatant segregation.

It said on the poster that people might be arrested — and I remember standing in front of the bulletin board and thinking: I'm making a major decision about my life here, because if I do this, there are a lot of people in my life who will not approve and it will have all of these consequences. And I remember there not being a shadow of doubt in my mind that I was going to go on this demonstration.

I went on the demonstration and it was all parents and children, about 10% of the people there were Swarthmore students. We were indeed rounded up roughly by the police and we were taken down to the county jailhouse. They said, "All kids are going to go to the bathroom." They took the kids out and they never came back, they disappeared. The parents were hysterical. We were shipped out that night to a state prison because it was too crowded in the county jail — and the state prison was segregated — there were black wings and white wings. So when we went into the lobby of the women's prison, we linked arms and they couldn't separate us into the two wings. So they put us in the day room and locked the door and we spent the night sleeping on the floor in the day room.   *Cathy*

Cathy Wilkerson, 1967

By 1964, more SDS members had become involved in civil rights work, some going to the South, and were learning firsthand about segregation and injustice.

I was on my first trip, helping drive and deliver things to civil rights projects in the South. On the one hand, it was every sixteen-year-old's Jack Kerouak fantasy. Here I am, we're getting shot at, which I thought, in my stupidity at the time, was great fun — which shows how little sense I had at the time. The danger involved didn't really register.

We were on our way out of Mississippi, we were actually in Kentucky, we had gotten through Tennessee. We were pretty much relaxed, we were out of the South, we thought. We get to a truck stop. I stopped in the restroom and apparently we'd been followed and a couple of guys just really beat me up pretty badly in the restroom — I cracked a rib. Talk about literally getting caught with your pants down. I got myself together, cleaned myself up as best I could, and walked into the truck stop. My friends took one look at me, put some money on the counter, got me out of there, and we got in the truck.

We'd gotten about three miles away and the engine exploded — and fire is shooting up into the cab of the truck, through the area where the gearshift is. It was a cold, rainy night. We put the engine fire out, it wasn't a really bad fire, but our truck was completely disabled. I was feeling pretty bad. And I suddenly realized for the first time how serious it was to really be about change in this country — and the risks this meant taking.

We stayed in the truck that night because we had nowhere else to go. We were waiting to see if people were going to come and get us and the three of us were just scared to death. In the morning somebody hiked to a phone booth and called up Dick Gregory, the black comedian and social activist, and he wired us enough money for a rental car and we got the heck out of there.

Mark

We got to Jackson and the next day there was a demonstration planned. We didn't exactly know what we were getting in for, we had just gotten there, and we were in a mass demonstration and we ended up in jail. The white women were taken to the county jail and I was in jail with about eighteen other women — white, northern women — for ten days. It was very different from San Francisco — there were police dogs, there were terrifying Mississippi police officers. This was not a liberal town.

We were all dispersed throughout Mississippi. I ended up in Leake County, which was right next to Philadelphia, where Schwerner, Cheney, and Goodman had been killed.* And I was sent out to the rural area, to this

---

*Michael Schwerner, James Chaney, and Andrew Goodman were three civil rights workers who were killed in Mississippi in June 1964. Their bodies were found, buried deep under an earthen dam, 44 days after they disappeared.

little shack on Red Dog Road, and we were told to organize for school integration, voter registration, and to try to set up a summer Freedom School.

I felt like I had gone to an underdeveloped country. It was a completely different world. And particularly on Red Dog Road. There was no electricity, the electricity stopped where the white community stopped. There were no paved streets, it was all dirt roads. People lived in little shacks. It was desperately poor. And there had never been a white person staying with any of these families before.   *Vivian*

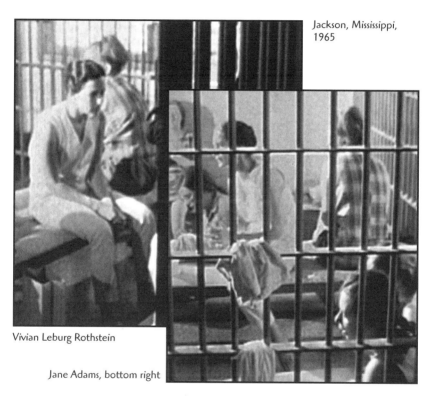

Jackson, Mississippi, 1965

Vivian Leburg Rothstein

Jane Adams, bottom right

Working in the South was hard and often dangerous — but it also had it's rewards.

In the South, in the 'freedom movement,' there was an unleashing of a tremendous optimism that we could remake the world — and that we could remake the world towards human equality. The core of the movement was a reconstructing of human relationships so that they would not be built on power and domination and exploitation but that they would be based on respect and mutual recognition.   *Jane*

MISSISSIPPI FREEDOM DEMOCRATIC PARTY

Voting was a key issue in the South, where legal restrictions and very real intimidation and violence meant that few blacks could vote or even dared to register.

In the summer of 1964, SNCC and CORE (Congress of Racial Equality) brought 1000 primarily white students, including SDS members, to Mississippi to help register voters, run Freedom Schools, and help build a Mississippi Freedom Democratic Party.

Black people didn't have the right to vote in the South, and they didn't have entree into the political party. There was only one political party, the Democratic Party, and the blacks weren't a part of it. They hadn't been a part of the political structure since right after Reconstruction. The Mississippi Freedom Democratic Party [MFDP] was a parallel party. It was parallel to the white party, which was the regular Democratic Party. It was an integrated party. Whites were welcome.

The MFDP sponsored some 'freedom votes' in which ballot boxes, cardboard boxes, were placed in churches and juke joints and gas stations — any place there was some free space where black people weren't afraid to walk in and mark on a piece of paper and put it in a box. Thousands and thousands of these ballots in which black people indicated they wanted to vote were rounded up.   *Casey*

One of the things I did in Mississippi was to canvas for the Mississippi Freedom Democratic Party. Going around and canvassing and signing people up was a first step in building a parallel institution, so that we could demonstrate that thousands of black people wanted to vote, would vote if given the vote. It made a lie of what white folks said about black folks being happy and content and it gave a somewhat safer way for many people, who were not yet willing to risk everything, to put their name on the card and say, "I want my freedom — and I will vote, if I get the vote."   *Jane*

The Democratic Party had always had a deep, deep contradiction; it was the party of liberals, the party of equality, justice, social justice — and it was built on the basis of segregation, because it could not exist without the 'solid South.' It was an unholy compromise.   *Jane*

From the beginning of SDS we'd had an uneasy relation to liberals. We included them in the formal language of the SDS membership card: "SDS is an organization of liberals and radicals. . . ." We recognized that they had influence and that they had values that we often approved of. We also thought that they had become corrupted by comfort and power and that they were too cozy with the establishment — or, in some cases, were the establishment. So we were on this uneasy knife-edge.   *Todd*

When we went to Atlantic City we went with the idea, as I understood it, that we, in fact, were the legitimate Democratic Party, that the white Democratic Party, by its policies of racial exclusion and racial supremacy, was not the heir to the traditions of the Democratic Party — and that the Democratic Party must, on a moral basis, recognize that the Mississippi Freedom Democratic Party represented the Democratic Party in Mississippi.
                                                                          Jane

We had a full set of delegates which we sent to the Democratic Party convention at Atlantic City and we asked that they be seated. It was the first time that we had chosen a liberal institution as the focus for our attacks. Heretofore we had chosen segregated lunch counters, the bad white guys, the Southerners. This was a national liberal organization which we had some hope would be on our side.   *Casey*

So, we get to Atlantic City and there's all this back-door deal-making and running around — and the upshot of it is that a great compromise is reached where the MFDP is going to be given two 'observer' seats — in somebody else's delegation, it wasn't even in the Mississippi delegation. It wasn't hard to see that it made a mockery of everything that we were about. And then Fannie Lou Hamer electrified the nation — in one of those clips you see over and over now — where an uneducated, untutored women from the South, who was a sharecropper who'd been beaten to within an inch of her life, gets up and says: we're here for our freedom, we're here for our rights, we aren't here for some crumbs off the table.

It was, in terms of the movement, a real watershed because it exposed the liberal establishment, for what it was — profoundly hypocritical and willing to get into bed with the devil if it took that to take care of some other pieces of the agenda. This was unacceptable.   *Jane*

Fannie Lou Hamer and Tom Hayden, 1965

So what seemed to be the rejection of the Mississippi Freedom Democratic Party in favor of what seemed to be a racist all white, pro-Goldwater as it turned out, Dixiecrat establishment was a blow. And what this rejection seemed to signal was that an incremental alliance strategy, what was then called 'coalition politics,' was a pipe-dream and that in some sense we'd have to go it alone.   *Todd*

The 1964 election posed a dilemma for SDS, and the question was: What was the worst threat: — Barry Goldwater and the right wing or was it Lyndon Johnson? It became one of those ideological divides as to who was the main enemy. Was it the liberals or was it the right? That debate continued on in different forms for many years.   *Steve*

There was put before SDS the proposition that we should half-heartedly endorse Lyndon Johnson for election under the slogan: Part of the Way with LBJ. I opposed it. It felt to me after the Gulf of Tonkin resolution and Atlantic City that we should not be in the business of supporting LBJ, even in a half-hearted way — and as a result I didn't even vote for president. It was the first year I could have voted legally, but I didn't vote for president.   *Todd*

In 1964, Congress passed the Civil Rights Act, followed in 1965 by the Voting Rights Act. Those laws went a long way toward outlawing legal segregation and discrimination. They also redirected attention and energy to other areas.

INTERRACIAL MOVEMENT OF THE POOR

Experiences in the civil rights movement, North and South, broadened many people's ideas about justice and equality.

The civil rights movement was raising issues of economics — unemployment and poverty and housing — not just civil rights in the South. We suddenly realized it would be possible to join it in the North but it would be a broader movement. It would be interracial.   *Tom*

SDS had been searching for a program that would provide a direct action outlet for students so it wouldn't be known just as this intellectual group from the North talking a lot about things.   *Sharon*

One of the fascinating things about SDS's early organizational structure was that if people had ideas about action programs, they were given space to develop that. Instead of passing resolutions, the tendency in SDS was to say, "If you want to do something, do it as an experimental project and see how far you can go organizing it." ERAP was the main one.   *Dick*

Sharon Jeffrey (right), Cleveland, 1964

A group of us had been urging SDS to set up projects in the North that would be supportive of what had been going on in the South, that would give an alternative for students in the North from having to run down to the South — and also accept that we had problems in the North and we, as Northerners, needed to begin to address those.   *Sharon*

Inspired by SNCC, SDS, through its Economic Research and Action Project (ERAP), began its own community organizing projects in northern cities in 1964.

So we chose nine different cities that we would go into and begin to organize an interracial movement of the poor.   *Sharon*

I walked into the SDS office in New York and from that point my life changed. I can remember sitting on the desk, literally seeing mice run through the office and Lee [Webb] talking about the civil rights movement, about the idea of an interracial movement of poor people, and about student involvement — and it was like I had found home. Everything that I had been thinking, feeling, for several years just began to fall into place. And they were planning ERAP, the Economic Research and Action Project. So I signed on.   *Carol*

> ERAP aims to stimulate a broadly-based interracial movement among those Americans who are now denied the opportunity to participate fully in the country's economic and political life.
>
> ERAP organizers work with poor people who are struggling to create their own organizations capable of protesting economic and social injustices . . . .
>
> Central to Economic Research and Action Project is the assumption that poor people — Negro and white — can be organized around economic and political grievances, and that there is a natural alliance among all poor in their common need for jobs, income, and control of their lives. This program is motivated by a belief that fundamental rearrangement of American priorities are needed if the problems of poverty are to be solved.   *ERAP brochure, 1966*

I had decided I was going to go back down to the South. Tom [Hayden] came up to Amherst to give a speech and came to talk to me — he was recruiting people to come to Newark. He told me that the civil rights move-ment was over in the South and the action was going to be in the North, so I should come to the North. And as he talked, it made a lot of sense. *Junius*

Junius Williams (left), Newark, 1965

It was almost like the lottery. We did a little analysis of the cities in the United States that had the biggest poverty problems and then sat around and figured who was going to go there. I had never been in Newark before in my life, but I got in a car with a bunch of people and we moved to Newark — and spent four years there, living on nothing, going door-to-door, trying to organize block clubs.   *Tom*

It was the first chance I had to really confront the harder problems of eco-nomics and race together — it was a class and race thing. Up to that point I had only been dealing with race problems— that's what the civil rights movement was all about. But if you didn't have a job and you couldn't afford that hamburger, what difference did it make whether you were sitting in the front of the restaurant or the back or in the restaurant at all. So this was the next logical step.   *Junius*

I can remember just knocking on the doors: knock, knock, and the lady would answer the door and I'd say, "Hey, I'm Casey Hayden, I'm with JOIN here and we're talking to people in the neighborhood who are on welfare about their problems with welfare. Could we talk to you?"   *Casey*

We would go door-to-door on a block, so thoroughly and so committedly. And we'd have about 25 seconds to connect with the person who answered the door. And we learned how to be compelling, warm, engaging — and our idea was to try to find out what that person's issues were and what they might want to come together with their neighbors to work on.   *Vivian*

Jesse Allen and Carol Glassman, Newark, 1964

Newark Community Union Project (NCUP) office

My first introduction to Newark was walking down the block with Jesse Allen, who was a local man, and knocking on people's doors and saying that we were from that office down on the corner that had the big picture of the rat in the window and we would do housing violation forms. We had taken the city's housing code, which was not enforced, and said to people that, if they were interested, we would file with the Housing Department what violations they had in their apartment. And we did that. We were after a way of getting to know people and beginning to bring them together.   *Carol*

Tom Hayden, Terry Jefferson, Jesse Allen, Carl Wittman in NCUP office, 1964

Phil Hutchings and Junius Williams (right), Newark, 1965

JOIN office,
Chicago, 1964

Todd Gitlin, Chicago, 1966

We were trying to get them to see that there was a bigger picture and that they could fit into it — and that they could change both the individual picture and the larger picture by participation.   *Junius*

It was door-knocking, it was organizing meetings, that really hard work of engaging with someone, sitting at their kitchen table. I learned a lot. It affected how I've done everything in my life since then — how to organize, how to build leadership, how to be the person behind, in the background, that empowers people to have a voice.   *Vivian*

Terry Jefferson and Tom Hayden, Newark, 1964

Poverty issues and civil rights issues and economic issues were all intertwined — and so it was very important to us to know organizers and to know people from other communities. So some people from our staff and some local people went to Mississippi and spent time with people in SNCC. And people from SNCC came to Newark. We were doing the same thing, in different communities.   *Carol*

We decided it would be useful to bring together all the people from the nine cities and from the black communities in the South. Since what we were about was creating an interracial movement of the poor, it would be useful for them to meet each other and for that group to begin to form itself as some kind of a political unit that would have an effect on the country.   *Sharon*

Poor People's Conference,
Cleveland, 1965

Carol Glassman, right

Poor People's Conference,
Newark, 1966

We had a series of what we called 'poor people's conferences.' The first one was in Cleveland, the next one was in Newark. At the Cleveland conference we brought a busload of people from Newark. There were people from Cleveland, from Chicago, from Hazard, Kentucky, and some SNCC people came — Fannie Lou Hamer was there. That contact, and sharing, and a sense of connection to a national movement was always very much in our minds, and in our thoughts, and in our hearts. So while I might have been walking on Peshine Avenue in Newark and knocking on a particular door, I saw myself, and felt myself, as part of something much larger than that. Bringing black people from Newark to a conference where they met poor white people from Kentucky and from Chicago was extremely important in terms of helping them understand not only the racial basis of their oppression but also the class basis — that poverty was not just a black-white issue but also a class issue.   *Carol*

Over the next few years, several hundred people worked in these community organizing projects — some full time, some just for a summer.

I was the one who got organized by the people I was organizing. I mean, it really worked almost completely in the reverse because I was able to go into people's homes and learn about, first of all how people lived in a northern urban poverty center, but also how people thought and people's histories. And so I got an incredible education. I barely went to class that year.   *Cathy*

There were just two of us organizing women. The rest of the JOIN project was really around organizing unemployed younger people. The Jobs or Income Now guys, it turned out, had a complex relationship with the women I was trying to organize, so there were some internal contradictions on the project. One of the women I'd organized had a relationship with one of the guys that JOIN had organized and he was very violent, he was always beating her up. I wasn't even discussing this issue in JOIN proper. I couldn't organize the women in this setting and so I ended up leaving.   *Casey*

I came to Newark when I was 22 years old and I lived in Clinton Hill for four and a half years. And during that time I had friends, lovers, we really set down roots. I still have personal connections to people in my life now who were people I met in Newark at that time. There was very much of a community feeling in the neighborhood that we lived in. It was centered around people's houses — we had barbeques in the summer, there were a couple bars we hung out in, and we danced.   *Carol*

By 10 o'clock at night we were still organizing people. The scene might have changed, we may have gone from their front porch to the local bar, or we may have been in one of those interminable meetings by that time, but the energy was still going.   *Junius*

We all lived collectively and we ate together. I ate more bologna sandwiches than I could eat in a lifetime.

We worked very hard. We were organizing together, going on demonstrations together, going to meetings together, struggling together — but we were also playing together and hanging out together, so it was a very alive time. The music was very alive. The whole feeling was very alive.   *Carol*

Seven days a week, we organized. Twenty-four hours a day, we organized. We were very serious organizers. We intended to change the world — and our business and our life was about changing the world.   *Sharon*

APARTHEID: SEGREGATION IN SOUTH AFRICA

Focus on civil rights was not limited to this country. The white 'apartheid' regime in South Africa was built on extreme segregation and discrimination. To support the black opposition there, SDS focused on United States involvement. In the process we learned about power structure research.

We were learning how 'the system' worked — how banks operated, how banks and corporations were connected, how banks and corporations were connected to foreign policy. And we discovered that loans from the Chase Manhattan Bank and a number of other big American banks had played a part in shoring up the apartheid regime in South Africa after the massacre that had taken place in Sharpeville in 1960, and that these loans were coming up for renewal in 1965.   *Todd*

There wasn't in the early '60s any large anti-apartheid movement. One of the things that allowed apartheid to continue and not fall apart was getting money from the United States, millions of dollars. The largest and most important bank dealing with South Africa was Chase Manhattan. So we decided to have a sit-in at Chase Manhattan and the slogan was: "Chase Manhattan — Partner in Apartheid."   *Carolyn*

Chase Manhattan Bank, New York, March 19, 1965

BULLETIN

STUDENTS FOR A
DEMOCRATIC
SOCIETY

JANUARY 1965   Vol 3, No 4

CHASE MANHATTAN...
PARTNER IN APARTHEID

SIT-IN PLANNED

In a letter to the Chase Manhattan Bank signed by SDS President Paul Potter, SDS recently called on Chase Manhattan to "cease and desist" in its financial assistance to the racist government of the Union of South Africa. In the probable event that Chase Manhattan refuses to pull out of its multimillion dollar investments and loans, SDS has announced its intention to carry out a sit-in in the Chase Manhattan offices just off Wall Street in New York's financial district. The date set for this action will be Friday, March 19, two days before the fifth anniversary of the Sharpeville massacre.

(cont. p 14)

OVERVIEW OF THE

FSM

by ERIC LEVINE
   Berkeley SDS

From the beginning, the politically interested, who constitute a minority on the Berkeley campus, as they do in any population, were deeply disturbed by the Administration action restricting political expression. Berkeley had a larger share than most campuses of politically active students, which helps explain why so many students—over a thousand—were ready to devote the better part of their time sitting inside and outside Sproul Hall during the 32-hour demonstration, October 1 and 2.

Who were these students? A questionaire returned by over 600 of the October 1-2 demonstrators showed that over 70% belong to no campus political organization. Half had never before participated in any dem-

SDS TO SPONSOR
VIETNAM MARCH

Perhaps the most far-reaching decision to come out of the December National Council meeting was the decision to sponsor a Student March on Washington to call for the end of American intervention in the

(cont. p 14)

South Africa...

Traditionally, American protests against apartheid have been content with condemnation of the Verwoeld regime. They have left the impression that apartheid is a system "way off there over the ocean", rather than a system tied to hidden American and British interests, with U.S. financial institutions providing essential support for the social system that institutionalizes the brutality of Sharpeville. The SDS action against Chase Manhattan is directed at exposing those private and powerful financial interests whose operations typify "the higher immorality". And on the same day, SDS chapters will demonstrate at home and branch offices of other corporations that invest in South Africa.

The role of U.S. corporations and financial institutions in the South African economy is great, and has been particularly significant, perhaps decisive, in maintaining the South African regime since 1960. After the Sharpeville massacre of March, 1960, the subsequent declaration of independence of the Republic of South Africa, and South Africa's decision to go off the pound sterling, foreign capital began to flee the country. It looked for a while in 1961 as if the economy was on the verge of collapse. But the United States came to the rescue. The U.S. Government offered to help in the form of a new Atomic Energy Commission six-year contract for South African uranium, improving the Republic's trade balance. Equally significant, the eighty U.S. companies with investments in South Africa increased their investments in 1961 alone by $23 million. And $150,000,000 in dollar loans was extended to the South African government from U.S.-dominated financial institutions

Chase Manhattan Bank, New York, March 19, 1965

We chose as the day for this protest the anniversary of the Sharpeville Massacre, the demonstration for which Nelson Mandela was sent to prison. A lot of us, hundreds, went down and shut down the main Chase Manhattan Bank office for a day.   *Carolyn*

Maybe fifty of us participated in the sit-in — and were arrested and dragged off to jail.   *Todd*

Chase Manhattan Bank, New York, March 19, 1965
Carolyn Craven, Eric Craven, Nancy Hollander, Todd Gitlin

The police thought they would really get us and break our spirits and they arrested the men first. So that left all the women alone. They really thought we'd fall apart with the men gone — they really thought the demonstration would end. They were real wrong. We hung in there and we were finally all arrested and taken away to another jail.   *Carolyn*

Mike Davis had sent out a bulletin [from the SDS National Office] saying, "Don't worry about where you're going to stay — housing will be arranged by the New York Police Department."   *Todd*

But that wasn't the end of it. Like many other SDS ideas, this one also spread to other campuses.

We did our power structure research and analyzed all the banks in Lincoln, Nebraska, and which ones had investments in South Africa and apartheid.

There weren't many blacks in Nebraska, and those who were there were with the football team, the Cornhuskers, which is a big deal out there. So we went to the black guys on the football team and explained to them about apartheid in South Africa and a number of them decided to join. So here we were, our band of long-haired radicals along with these big guys, black guys from the University of Nebraska football team, leading our march on the banks through downtown Lincoln.   *Carl D*

We were really able to raise the issue of apartheid as an issue for a lot of people who had never even heard of it.   *Carolyn*

This was one pebble in what eventually became, twenty years on, an avalanche of attacks on American complicity with the regime in South Africa.   *Todd*

After years of struggle in South Africa, apartheid was finally ended. Nelson Mandela was released from prison in 1990 — and in 1994 he was elected president of South Africa.

4
Vietnam | *1965*

When I graduated from ninth grade, the graduation speaker was [Secretary of State] Dean Rusk, who had a kid in my graduating class. He held up a map of Indochina, as he called it, and said, "This little country is one you haven't heard of yet, but you will in the future." This was in 1962. And he said, "This is going to be an important country in the future, you should find out more about it." It piqued my curiosity.   *Sue*

In 1964, many in SDS were slowly becoming aware of a country called Vietnam.

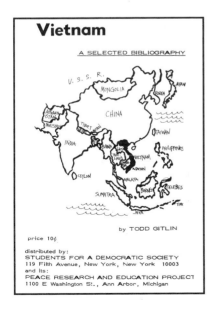

It's the fall of 1964. There are about 25,000 American soldiers, 'advisors', in Vietnam and we thought we were not going to be able to evade Vietnam, Vietnam was coming after us and we'd better get ready for it. The war was going to become central to SDS whether we liked it or not — and for the most part SDS didn't, because we had domestic concerns that we wanted to give priority.   *Todd*

We didn't want to become a single-issue organization, and if we emphasized the war, that's the path we were heading down.   *Carolyn*

I was in Newark feeling that here's the beginning of the end of our little war on poverty. We're knocking on doors trying to do something about landlords, rats, roaches, all this stuff. But more and more troops are being sent, the money is ratcheting up.

I thought that we were going to run into real troubles because of the lack of funding or commitment to the domestic problems of jobs and poverty because of the war.   *Tom*

Vietnam remained very back-burner until, at the beginning of August, 1964, came the claim that two American warships in the Gulf of Tonkin, right off Vietnam, had been fired upon by North Vietnamese gunboats. Big press conference, McNamara, Johnson, denunciation of the North's heinous crime — and bombardment, what was billed as retaliatory bombardment. This spurred Johnson to bring before Congress a resolution that basically assigned him carte blanche to do whatever he deemed necessary to do to protect American troops in Vietnam. This resolution was passed in the House of Representatives with no dissent and in the Senate with two dissents, long may their names live — Senator Wayne Morse and Senator Ernest Gruening.   *Todd*

I can remember listening to the radio as the country was dealing with the crisis in the Gulf of Tonkin and the president was ordering increased American involvement — and that order changed all of our lives.   *Carol*

MARCH ON WASHINGTON

Vietnam was a central topic of discussion at the December 1964 SDS National Council meeting.

Paul Booth and I decide that we should get I.F. Stone to come to the National Council meeting and tell SDS about Vietnam, which for the most part it doesn't know much about.   *Todd*

I.F. Stone was perhaps the leading left journalist of the time, he was the editor and publisher of *I.F. Stone's Weekly.*   *Dick*

He came and did give that talk.   *Todd*

After a long discussion, SDS decided to organize a march in Washington for April 17, 1965, to protest the escalating action in Vietnam.

I. F. Stone speaking at SDS National Council, December, 1964.

March '65, 150,000 ground troops go right into South Vietnam. We're now caught up in a discussion of: where is Vietnam and why are we doing this? Zero people in the United States knew anything about Vietnam or where it was.   *Tom*

At the time, I had no idea where Vietnam was. Paul Cowan got out this map and showed us where Vietnam was. We started studying about what was happening in Southeast Asia.   *Marilyn*

It was very early on. At that point there was very little support for the anti-war movement and tremendous reaction to people who spoke up. I mean, this was a country that had almost unanimous support for WW II and for the Korean War and the thought of attacking a government policy around a war was just outrageous.   *Cathy*

Steve Weissman came to town and said he was organizing for an SDS March on Washington against the war. He needed a place to crash so we said, "Come stay at our place." And he started talking to us about SDS. He said SDS was different than other left groups — it comes out of a whole different tradition. They're all related to the different splits in the communist movement and socialist movement in Europe while SDS identifies more with the IWW and American radicalism. This was music to our ears. The next week I was off to Washington.   *Carl D*

Lo and behold, this demonstration came to pass and was much larger than any of us had expected. We thought that maybe there would be 3000 people. It was dazzling to be able to bring 25,000 people to Washington.
                                                                                      Todd

Washington DC, April 17, 1965

After hours of picketing the White House we went down to the Washington monument and had our rally.   *Todd*

Washington DC, April 17, 1965

Senator Ernest Gruening speaking at rally, April 17, 1965.

The most important thing about the rally was that it took place. There were also symbols that mattered. Senator Gruening was there, one of the honorable men who had voted against the Tonkin Gulf resolution. The war was horrible, he said. That mattered, coming from him. I.F. Stone was there, he had helped set us on the course of concern about Vietnam, he told us some history. That mattered. From the civil rights movement, Bob Moses of SNCC, an honorable figure. He was there to remind us that there were connections, that what went on in the American south was not discon-nected from what America's role was in the world.   *Todd*

By far the most powerful speech was a speech by Paul Potter, our president at the time. Paul Potter's talk was the galvanizing moment when a New Left position was launched — about the war, about honor, about decency, about the need to transform the country in some enormous way. It was ringing. It was the purest possible expression of the SDS mood.   *Todd*

Most of us grew up thinking that the United States was a strong but humble nation, that involved itself in world affairs only reluctantly, that respected the integrity of other nations and systems, and that engaged in wars only as a last resort . . .

The incredible war in Vietnam has provided the razor, the terrifying sharp cutting edge, that has finally severed the last vestige of illusion that morality and democracy are the guiding principles of American foreign policy. . . . The further we explore the reality of what this country is doing and planning in Vietnam the more we are driven towards the conclusion of Senator Morse that the United States may well be the greatest threat to peace in the world today. That is a terrible and bitter insight for people who grew up as we did—and our revulsion at that insight, our refusal to accept it as inevitable or necessary, is one of the reasons that so many people have come here today.   *Paul Potter, SDS president, April 17, 1965*

The cherry trees were in bloom and everything was white. It was beautiful and I was lying on the ground when Paul spoke and I remember his speech and I remember realizing that this was a turning point.   *Casey*

What kind of a system is it that justifies the United States or any country in seizing the destinies of other people and using them callously for its own purposes? What kind of a system is it that disenfranchises people in the South, that leaves millions and millions of people throughout this country impoverished and excluded from the mainstream and promise of American Society, . . . that consistently puts material values before human values? What kind of a system is that?

We must name that system. We must name it, describe it, analyse it, understand it, and change it *Paul Potter, April 17, 1965*

I went to that march and I was just overwhelmed. I was convinced that as a result of that march the war was going to end the next day. We really believed in a lot of the civic ideas we got from our high school civics textbooks that American democracy worked relatively well and if we just went out and protested and mobilized enough people things would change relatively quickly. It was a source of radicalization to us that the more we protested, the more they escalated the war. As time went on we began to get a more and more sophisticated analysis of what we were really up against.

Carl D

There is no simple plan, no scheme or gimmick that can be proposed here. There is no simple way to attack something that is so deeply rooted in the society. If the people of this country are to end the war in Vietnam, and to change the institutions which created it, then the people of this country must create a massive social movement—and if that can be built around the issue of Vietnam, then that is what we must do. *Paul Potter, April 17, 1965*

Paul Potter, 1965

VIGIL AT THE LBJ RANCH

Not all SDS members went to Washington that day.

Lyndon Johnson, the president of the United States, lived not too very far from Austin, Texas, so we decided that instead of trying to get anybody to go to Washington, we would go to Lyndon Johnson's ranch.   *Robert*

We didn't want the president to be able to leave Washington and not feel an anti-war presence — in other words, retreat to Texas and not have anything happen.   *Alice*

Our idea was that we were going to go and tell LBJ what we thought about the war. They wouldn't let us in. They closed the gate.   *Judy*

Jeff Shero and Alice Embree outside President Johnson's ranch, April 17, 1965

Outside President Johnson's ranch, April 17, 1965.

And so it was Sunday and we showed up, about 40 of us, with signs, and had a silent vigil outside Ranch Road 1, with the Secret Service and the Department of Public Safety and all manner of law enforcement personnel.

A long time later I learned that the march had had a very big impact on the president. It was something that had come right to his front door. This was his retreat, this was where he took foreign dignitaries and his cabinet — and all of a sudden, right there in the middle of the Texas hill country, we showed up saying he should end the war.   *Alice*

SDS GROWS

After the march on Washington, students across the country wanted to know what was this war in Vietnam — and what was SDS.   *Robert*

The organization just mushroomed then, and it wasn't that we were doing anything really different. It was like putting a barrel under a rain spout. People just came pouring into it.   *Steve*

We had this fledgling SDS chapter, a few people, maybe 30. We advertised a meeting to organize for a march against the war and we got one of these small meetings rooms at the University of Chicago — and 120 people showed up. "Where can we buy tickets for the bus?" This was a constituency that was ready to take off.   *Bob*

We were now suddenly surrounded by these thousands of people whom we had organized — so there was the sense that we happy few were no longer going to be few. The success of organizing this demonstration meant we were now immersed in, if not leading, a mass movement. What are we going to do with all these people? What do they know about us? They think we're an anti-war organization.   *Todd*

After the march we were going to have a National Council meeting and I remember walking into the room and for the first time I didn't know three-quarters of the people in the room. I had no idea who they were. They were from all over, places I'd never heard of, colleges I'd never heard of — and it was clear that on that day SDS became a different organization.
                               Carolyn

SDS almost instantly went from being a rather obscure organization to a very public organization, a very visible organization.

We're no longer this face-to-face organization where everybody knows everybody else by first name. We've slept together, we've joshed together, we've eaten together — we are this sort of 'beloved community' in small. And now suddenly we're in this three-ring circus. So there was both this thrill of achievement and, at the same time, this bewilderment and some apprehension about what was going to break up our old gang.   *Todd*

SDS National Council meeting, September, 1963, Bloomington, Indiana.
Left to right: Tom Hayden, Don McKelvey, Jon Seldin, Nada Chandler, Nancy Hollander, Steve Max, Dan Millstone, Vernon Grizzard, Paul Booth, Carl Wittman, Mary McGroarty, Steve Johnson, Lee Webb, Sarah Murphy, Todd Gitlin, Dick Flacks, Mickey Flacks, Robb Burlage, Rennie Davis

Many of those who joined SDS at that time did so because of Vietnam. In 1965, Carl Oglesby was supporting his family by working as a technical writer for the Bendix Corporation.

At Bendix we had a project called 'Jungle Canopy' and the outward purpose of the Jungle Canopy project was to find out, for pure meteorological reasons, what size of raindrop, or 'particulate of mist' — I remember that phrase — would fall to what level of the jungle canopy. The real purpose was to find out how to run the defoliation program. They wanted to know: should they dispense this poison, Agent Orange and the others, should they dispense it in a raindrop sized droplet or should it be as a mist? Discovering that, I can't tell you, just devastated me. I'm saying, "What, we don't do things like that, we're the good guys."

I had written a play called *The Peacemaker* centered on an actual character named Dyke Garret, who actually tried to stop the Hatfield-McCoy feud in Kentucky. I was interested in the question: if you know something bad is going to happen and there doesn't really seem to be any way to stop it, do you have a moral obligation to try to stop it anyway. It was for me, in retrospect, an interesting question because it became very personal as the war in Vietnam loomed up and finally began to confront me with the same issue I had tried to confront my character with. That play was produced in 1964 at the University of Michigan.

An SDS chapter member named Roger Manela went to see the play and also discovered this statement of mine on the Vietnam war. Roger called me and said he thought he knew all the radicals on campus and he wondered what I thought of SDS. I said, "What's SDS?" He asked if he could come out to explain SDS to me and within the hour here comes Roger on his Harley-Davidson tooling up Sunnyside Street. The long and the short of it is that I liked Roger a lot and was very open to his thought that I should get involved in SDS or at least get to know the SDS people.   *Carl O*

Carl Oglesby at SDS convention, June, 1965

The reason I liked the SDS kids so much was their openness, their interest in real discussion of issues and not just confronting one another with pat positions that had already been worked out and were not going to be changed for anything. People were listening to each other, hearing what each other had to say, and were, I thought, extraordinarily sophisticated about the range of social issues that had to be dealt with in looking at the country in that period. I was delighted to find kindred spirits.   *Carl O*

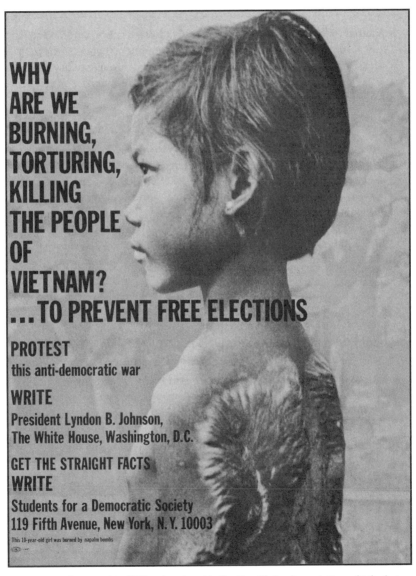

WHY ARE WE BURNING, TORTURING, KILLING THE PEOPLE OF VIETNAM? ...TO PREVENT FREE ELECTIONS

PROTEST
this anti-democratic war

WRITE
President Lyndon B. Johnson,
The White House, Washington, D.C.

GET THE STRAIGHT FACTS
WRITE
Students for a Democratic Society
119 Fifth Avenue, New York, N.Y. 10003

This 10-year-old girl was burned by napalm bombs

Poster originally printed in 1965 to be placed in the New York subway stations. At the last minute, the NY Transit Authority refused to allow the posters on the walls of the subway. SDS later won in court but by then the posters had all been given to chapters and used in many demonstrations.

SDS had a big beautiful powerful poster about Vietnam and what did it say: for the true facts, write SDS and it gave the address. And SDS had nothing to respond with, so I got involved.   *Carl O*

> Vietnam is the ground of an absolute Cold War confrontation. Not just the tactics or even the strategy but the underlying world-view, the great tormented metaphysics of American foreign policy has there brought itself again to the brink of its inherent consequences. We will try to reach into the heart of this torment.
>
> The crisis has been building since 1954. But it was the US action of February 7, 1965 that precipitated the present, more harrowing phase. On that date, US and South Vietnamese aircraft bombed North Vietnam. . . . The war had been widened. Through March and early April, it continued to widen. Air attacks crept further toward Hanoi and the northern industrial and population centers. US combat troops were introduced. There was growing pressure in Washington for a major ground-force commitment, perhaps 350,000 men.   *Carl Oglesby,* The Vietnam War: World Revolution and American Containment *(SDS pamphlet), 1965*

TEACH-INS

About that time, faculty at the University of Michigan, trying to find something they could do to oppose the war, came up with the idea of a 'teach-in' — and the idea of teach-ins quickly spread and became a favorite tool of SDS chapters. Forty years later, 'teach-ins' are still used in many ways today.

The faculty group decided that they should do something about the war too. And what they decided to do was on a given day they would devote their classes to the question of the Vietnam War. This was publicized. The right wing heard about it and went into orbit: this is a public institution, these teachers are paid out of the public coffers, it's a violation of their sacred trust, etc., etc. Huge outcry which, in retrospect, was perfect for us because it absolutely galvanized the entire campus and made people, even physical education majors, think about the war in Vietnam.

The university decreed that the day of teaching about Vietnam was not going to happen and any teacher who dared do that would be summarily axed or some bad thing would happen. So the faculty decided — by this time the group had grown rather large — to propose that they teach their regular daytime classes as usual but that in the evening, at night, there would be what they dared call a 'teach-in' on Vietnam. This was exactly what should have happened from our standpoint. The argument about it raised the ante like crazy, got hundreds or thousands more people interested in what was happening. And the idea of doing the teaching at night created the sense that this was something really special, that something extraordinary was happening in the world — and that you had to do irregular things to come to terms with it.

I had by that time been studying Vietnam and knew the literature better than most other people and I got drawn into it. I did some of the teaching at the teach-in.   *Carl O*

It had a sense of an ongoing seminar, a rolling seminar, that had lots of participation and had lots of people both speaking and asking and inquiring and wondering. And I remember a certain sense of carnival, like any gathering of young people coming together with no rules and no boundaries. So we went all night — and you could go from room to room and you could go listen to a debate between people or you could go to talk about tactics.   *Bill*

Flyer for first teach-in, Ann Arbor, Michigan, March 1965

At the end of it we all gathered at the Michigan Union and there was a kind of an outdoor rally. That was the teach-in, and the idea — to call it wild-fire understates it, it spread so fast. And not only nationally but internationally.

Carl O

As soon as that happened, those of us on other campuses wanted to do the same thing and it wasn't long before we organized something very similar at the University of Chicago — and this happened at hundreds of universities.

Those were the days when a lot of students were really in awe of powerful intellectuals so part of the teach-in, maybe in Ann Arbor too, but in Chicago was that these really world-famous minds were up on the platform telling people they had the right to be angry and opposed to this war. So that's like a one-way message. But, of course, as good SDSers we wanted to create a different kind of experience which was much more egalitarian with small group meetings, different kinds of workshops on different issues that were not just to inform about the issues but I'm sure there were some action-oriented workshops — what can we do.

Dick

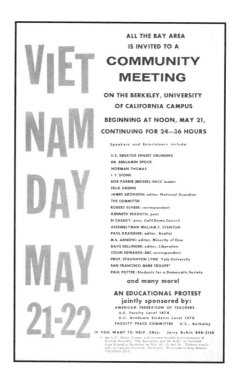

We couldn't get seats at all, we had to stand up for hours. And they would go on, I don't remember how long. They went on at least 24 hours, sometimes they went on for 48. And like filibusters in Congress, one person would go home and go to sleep, somebody else would stand up and give a speech. They'd get done, somebody else would stand up and give a speech. And this was where we learned what was going on in Vietnam.

Just as my views about civil rights had been formed by my social studies classes at Woodrow Wilson High School, so had my views of foreign policy. And we had been told by our president, several in a row as a matter of fact, that we were bringing democracy to South Vietnam, that's what we were doing. And what the teach-ins did was examine that basic principle.

The next teach-in I went to, I heard the word imperialism for the first time — that a country that wants to impose its ideas of democracy on another country, a country that is interested, perhaps, in the oil that lies underneath their soil, might have other interests besides just democracy in mind, and might actually be there for motives that weren't good, that weren't beneficial to the people involved. And that was just the beginning. And from there, my curiosity — and that of all the rest of us — about what was really going on was piqued. I wanted to know more.   *Mike*

The idea was that you need to have a debate between various points of view and that, of course, we would come out on top because we were right.

Jane

I heard one of the senators or one of his staff people say that if they can't win a debate in Salt Lake City about the war in Vietnam then they're in deep trouble. And the long and the short of it is that at least those who came to hear the debate — and the place was packed, people were hanging from the rafters — the sentiment was overwhelmingly with us critics.   *Carl O*

We decided to start things off with a bang by organizing a teach-in on the war in Vietnam. Lo and behold, the state legislature, which is right there in Lincoln, got all in a tizzy and all the newspapers put banner headlines: Teach-in comes to the University of Nebraska. Again, all this enormous pressure came upon us to not just present the radical point of view, we had to get somebody from the State Department. Our response was, "Fine, get him up there!" We loved to have a go at them.

A few weeks after we had the teach-in, I had this knock at my door in downtown Lincoln, Nebraska, and I opened it up and there was this great big huge guy standing there wearing bib overalls and a flannel shirt and he says, "Are you the Carl Davidson who organized that teach-in against Vietnam at the university?" And I looked at this guy and said, "Oh shit — yeah, that's me." And he says, "Well, my name is Arlo Hoppe and I'm from the US Farmers Association and we're chartering a bus to go to the fall march on Washington to protest the Vietnam War and I've got to get my crops in and I can't go so I'd like you to go in my place — and I'll buy you a ticket!"   *Carl D*

The idea of the campus having the ability to have that much impact on political events was one of the great ideas that came out of it — that teachers and students weren't just members of an inward-turned enclave that had no way to have an impact on ordinary society. No, the institution of the university, and colleges, was a powerful institution and could , in this way, find itself playing a major role in a major national struggle.   *Carl O*

The idea that people were together with faculty, graduate students, and under-graduates working together in this new way, at this new time of day, in this new framework, I think, was tremendously liberating for those of us who were part of it. And I think that's part of the appeal of this mode of action, part of why it did spread around the country — and probably helped feed later developments called 'free universities' and alternative educational models. Remember, we did this — we actually could do intellectual work in a different way than the traditional classroom and teacher-as-expert model.

And down to the present day, we have teach-in movements around various issues on American campuses. *Dick*

NOVEMBER 1965

SDS, after the April March on Washington, was tired of national marches, and there was even a feeling that aside from generating some publicity, they might not be worth all that much politically. But then the Committee for a Sane Nuclear Policy, SANE, called for a march against the war to be held that November.

The SANE people needed SDS to be involved or their march would be a bust and they knew it, so SANE offered SDS the opportunity to have somebody make a speech so that our point of view would get across. I was president of SDS so it fell on me to figure out what to say. *Carl O*

> This country, with its thirty-some years of liberalism, can send 200,000 young men to Vietnam to kill and die in the most dubious of wars, but it cannot get 100 voter registrars to go into Mississippi. What do you make of it?
>
> The financial burden of the war obliges us to cut millions from an already pathetic War on Poverty budget. But in almost the same breath Congress appropriates one hundred forty million dollars for the Lockheed and Boeing companies to compete with each other on the supersonic transport project. . . . What do you make of it?
>
> *Carl Oglesby,* Let Us Shape the Future, *November, 1965*

I drafted a speech, then the night before the demonstration read the speech to a group of SDSers and spent the night working over it with anybody who wanted to get involved. The first group was 30-40 folks and then out of that group 6-10 or so decided to stay up all night with me and work on the thing. By the next day we had a speech which was really a collective effort in the best sense of the word. *Carl O*

Let me then speak directly to humanist liberals. . . . Corporatism or humanism: which? For it has come to that. Will you let your dreams be used? Will you be grudging apologists for the corporate state? Or will you help try to change it—not in the name of this or that blueprint or ism, but in the name of simple human decency and democracy and the vision that wise and brave men saw in the time of our own Revolution.

And if your commitment to human values is unconditional, then disabuse yourselves of the notion that statements will bring change, if only the right statements can be written, or that interviews with the mighty will bring change if only the mighty can be reached, or that marches will bring change if only we can make them massive enough, or that policy proposals will bring change if only we can make them responsible enough.

We are dealing now with a colossus that does not want to be changed. It will not change itself. It will not cooperate with those who want to change it. Those allies of ours in the government — are they really our allies? If they are, they don't need advice, they need constituencies; they don't need study groups, they need a movement. And if they are not, then all the more reason for building that movement with a most relentless conviction.

Carl Oglesby, Let Us Shape the Future, *November, 1965*

5
Organizing

As SDS grew, some left school to travel around the country organizing other students, continuing the slow process of building a movement — one person, one campus, one demonstration at a time.

I entered into the crazy life of a full-time organizer around the war, going to campus after campus, back and forth across the country, watching the crowds grow.   *Carl O*

Carl Oglesby

There was a rally in NY at Washington Square at which I gave a short little talk against the war. The rally finally broke up and, with a few other people, I was walking to the subway stop and five or six right-wing kids jumped us — and clobbered us pretty hard. I got punched right in the face by this guy who came out of nowhere. And then as quickly as they had hit us, they were gone. The cops then showed up. I remember in the middle of it screaming, "Where are the cops now, where are the cops now?" because they'd been all over the place during the rally. Well, in a minute or so they showed up and they wanted to know if we wanted to press charges. And I said to this one cop, "I don't want to press charges, I want to talk to these kids." Before that the cops had no idea where the kids were, "Oh, we'll never catch them, they've disappeared." But as soon as I said we didn't want to press charges, we just wanted a discussion, they knew where the kids were.

So we went to the station house and a few minutes later the kids came in and for the next hour or so we SDSers sat at a table in the police station in New York, rapping about the war with these kids. And I can't say that we changed any of their minds, at least not right away, but I do think that we reached them. And I even think we reached a few of the cops. That seems to me a characteristically SDS kind of moment.   *Carl O*

It was a fertile time. I had an old station wagon with literature in the back. I was supposed to get a little money from the office and once in a while I'd get $10 or $15, it was really barely gas money. But I got literature and buttons and when you'd hit the campus you could sell those and have a little party and get a little money to get to the next place.

And you'd hit the campus and you'd usually have one name and this person would let you sleep on their floor. So you'd crash on their couch or floor. And they'd say, "Gee, SDS seems really great but you can't do anything here because this is the most conservative university."

I would spend about three days talking to people, seeing what was on peoples' minds, the issues, and saying, "Hey, we're going to have this SDS meeting and maybe you'd like to come." Typically towards the end of the week, we'd have a meeting and there'd be maybe 15–30 people. And there'd usually be some issue on the campus — frequently the draft was an issue. And I'd get up and talk about SDS and say this is a decentralized organization and if you make an SDS, you can make your own decisions. They'd talk a lot and usually form an SDS.   *Jeff*

Jeff Shero (center) organizing a protest

And then I'd say, "My experience is that a demonstration, a direct action, is really important and maybe we should do something." Action transforms peoples' lives. As soon as they saw they could do something, they were emboldened and empowered. And then that SDS chapter would roll.

And you'd get to the next university and they'd tell you that theirs was the most conservative of all and you'd start that whole process again.   *Jeff*

Death March demonstration in Austin, Texas, 1965

Death March demonstration in Austin, Texas, 1965

I went to campuses where we had no contacts at all. I walked around Texas Tech, and I couldn't spot anybody that I thought would be sympathetic to what I was there to talk about. I looked on the bulletin board to see if there were any meetings of any student organizations and there were none. Texas Tech is a long way from nowhere — Lubbock is out in the middle of West Texas — and the next nearest campus is probably 300 miles away. So I'm there for the night.   *Robert*

Robert Pardun, 1965

I took a stick and I made a little cardboard sign. And I wrote on the sign: SDS. And I attached the cardboard to the stick and I stuck the stick in the ground and I sat down next to it. And people would walk by and they would say, "What are you doing here? What is SDS anyway?" And I would tell them a little bit about what SDS was — and by the time school was over that afternoon, I had a place to sleep. After a couple of days, I've got five people, I've got a chapter at Texas Tech University.   *Robert*

At Utah State, which was controlled by the Mormons, we organized a 'smoke-in'. It was the only time I helped organize a smoke-in, but that was the issue on campus. The issue wasn't really smoking cigarettes — it was really an anti-Mormon control of the state university issue. Students sat down and smoked cigarettes and the university called the police and it got the SDS chapter rolling big time.   *Jeff*

My friend lent me an old '48 Cadillac hearse that I used to do a lot of campus traveling.   *Carl D*

A young couple from Ames, Iowa, who were young faculty members, had a TR-4 that they loaned me. It's hard to imagine now, how heady just that fact was, of being a woman driving around in this little sports car, a 'Make Love Not War' bumper sticker, out on these broad stretches of freeway in Iowa, Kansas, Nebraska, and Missouri.   *Jane*

Most of the kids out there were not as long-haired or scruffy as us. They were these earnest blond-as-could-be blue-eyed farm kids who had grown up in the church and had decent values and were just morally aghast at what was going on in the South at the time or the slaughter that was going on in Vietnam — and were open to listening to what we had to say.   *Carl D*

It's difficult to recall just how odd it was in many parts of the country to be opposed to the Vietnam war. SDS got an invitation to send a speaker to the University of Tulsa in the fall of 1965. By the time I got there not only was I banned from speaking on campus to oppose the war, but even a debate was not acceptable to the authorities. So I ended up speaking at a coffee-house in downtown Tulsa and there were 50–100 people. Most people then, and not only in Oklahoma, were still perfectly content with the war.   *Todd*

A guy named Stan Nadel put up a sign above a marine recruiter at the center of the University of Michigan campus, a place called the 'fishbowl' — and the sign was a long quote from the Nuremberg trials and then an arrow pointing at the marine recruiter saying: THIS MAN IS A WAR CRIMI-NAL. And the fishbowl just filled up with students — angry, debating, confused. Some thought what Nadel did was just horrendous and dreadful and there were fights and shouting matches and pushing in the fishbowl, and it went on for a week.   *Bill*

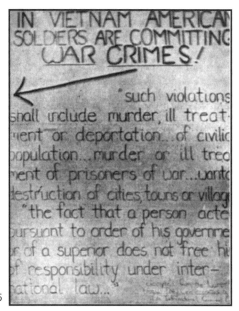

Stan Nadel's sign, September 1965

I learned more in that week about the war in Vietnam. I learned more history, I learned more facts, I learned more of the sociology and the politics of what was going on in the world than I'd ever learned before and maybe ever learned since. It was one week of intense political education — informal, in the hallways, in the streets — that was real political education.   *Bill*

We planned to show a Viet Cong film. All hell broke loose, the Pennsylvania State Legislature went into special session wanting to ban this. They decided to let us do it but it had to be a balanced program — they had to have people from the State Department doing the opposite side. We went to the auditorium, which held about 500 people, to show our film and it was packed. I was given the task of introducing the speaker. I'd never given speeches before and I got up before all these people and froze. I absolutely could not open my mouth. Finally my roommate came out and pulled me away and managed to give some kind of half-baked introduction to get the thing going.   *Carl D*

Carl Davidson, 1967

The program turned out to be a big success but I was very upset that I'd had this stage fright and couldn't give the speech at this crucial time. So my roommate and I decided to do something about it. We created a thing called the Hyde Park Forum where we got a big old wooden crate and painted 'SOAP' on it. There was this intersection on campus where every time classes changed, for about a fifteen-minute period, within shouting distance there were always about 500 people. And so we hid this big old soap box behind the bushes and whenever classes changed we'd drag it out, jump up on it and give speeches. We made this a speech training project for our whole little peace group. We all had to do it — we all had to learn speeches and not do what Carl did! So one outcome of my disaster at the opening of the Viet Cong film was I finally learned how to give a speech.   *Carl D*

What got me out of high school were some leaflets I had written at the end of 1965. Our high school principal had sent out a notice for a gift drive for our boys in Vietnam. I wrote up this leaflet that I handed out on campus saying if we really wanted to support them, we'd bring them home. The vice-principal of our high school kicked me out right away. That's when I began doing movement work full time.   *Mark*

What I remember most about my high school is that there is a 10-foot fence around it. In parts, there are three rows of barbed wire strung along the top. What concerns me most about the fence is not that it keeps me in—but that it keeps the rest of the world out, admitting only those portions of 'reality' which the administration deems safe for us to view. Those responsible for our education have done their utmost to create an artificial community on the high school campus; a community that will demonstrate to us that it is better to 'adjust' to an unsuitable society than to change the society into something in which we can live with dignity. If we are to lead meaningful lives, and do more than pass on our problems to the next generation, we shall have to break out of that artificial community.   *Mark Kleiman,* High School Reform, *1965*

Sue Eanet Klonsky at a demonstration in New York, 1965

I got recruited to come to New York City to work for SDS in the regional office — to work full-time organizing the office and doing outreach to new campuses. New York is just swarming with colleges and many of the community colleges, or two-year schools, had SDS chapters.   *Sue*

At the point that SDS was organizing national demonstrations, we were in the position of talking to people in the neighborhood about the war and about going to the demonstrations. Part of our involvement in anti-war activities was to stop the war. But it was also to make the connections between the choices that the government made about what was important and how it was going to use its resources and how those translated into things like unemployment, poor housing, and schools, and all the issues that were important to people.   *Carol, Newark ERAP project*

Statewide demonstration in Newark, New Jersey, organized by the Hoboken ERAP project, 1966

Although the chapters were the center of activity, it was really the connections among SDS members that were key. In addition to information in the SDS paper, first called the *SDS Bulletin* and later called *New Left Notes*, SDS members got together often and shared ideas, at national conventions and at a variety of other meetings.

Carl Wittman, Steve Max, Nancy Hollander at an SDS National Council meeting, 1963

Penny Chaloupka, Todd Gitlin, Dick Flacks, Tom Hayden, 1963

Bob Moore, Bob Ross, Dick Flacks, Rennie Davis, Rich Horowitz, 1964

There's all this incredible cross-pollination that's going on at these National Council meetings, some of which is happening in the workshops, some of which is happening at the plenaries on the floor, some of which is happening on the grass outside, or the talk sessions that go on half of the night, maybe people lined up in sleeping bags on a big floor and the conversation just continues across as some people are trying to go to sleep and other people can't because the ideas are just too exciting.   *Robert*

Paul Booth, SDS convention, 1965

Todd Gitlin and Mike Davis at SDS convention, Kewadin, Michigan, 1965

SDS meeting, 1965. Vernon Grizzard, vice-president 1964-5, second from left

A number of us from Austin had headed north for a national meeting up in the Chicago area. We left Austin, we picked up some people in Norman, Oklahoma, we picked up people at the University of Missouri and we were somewhere in Illinois and it was snowing like crazy. There was a blizzard. I think it snowed thirty-some inches by the time we got to Chicago. So we're driving down the highway, there was no traffic on the highway, only fools like us would be out on the highway on a day like this. And you can see only about 50 feet in front of the car.

And all of a sudden, on the side of the road is this figure, completely covered up, his face is under this pulled down coat. And he's hitch-hiking. So we come to a skidding stop on the other side of this person. The car is packed, there's more of us in the car than should be in the car as it is, but this guy's going to freeze to death if we don't pick him up. So we pull over to the side of the road, we open up the door, everyone piles in a little further, sitting on each other's laps. And in gets this guy with his big coat wrapped all around him and he pulls back his hood — and everybody says, "Chaz, where are you going?" And he says, "I'm going to the SDS meeting in Chicago just like you are." The only other fool on the road is one of us.

Robert

6
The Draft

As the war grew, draft calls also grew.

We always opposed the war but it became clear that one of the things we had to oppose was the draft, not just the war itself but specifically the draft, because this is where the young men were coming from.   *Carolyn*

Every young man had to register at age 18. If you were a student, early in that period, you got an automatic deferment.   *Bob*

Middle-class kids had the privilege of not serving and so there was this hugely disproportionate mass of low-income guys, kids of color, being drafted and coming back dead.   *Sue*

The US government has declared a war — unilaterally and unconstitutionally — on a place on the other side of the world that Americans know virtually nothing about, and they have the gall to think that you should simply abandon your life and go kill a bunch of people you've never heard of and run the risk of dying — because they say so.   *Todd*

In the Sixties, the voting age was 21. It was lowered to 18 in 1970.

A very important thing that people always forget is that we couldn't vote. It wasn't just that the people who were African-American in the South were shackled and disenfranchised by a system that said you can't vote, or you can't vote without putting your life in danger, but there were 4, 5, 6, 7 million American college students who couldn't vote. So when people today say, "Why did you work outside the system?" or, "What do you think about outside or inside the system?" it's a hilarious question to me since I was outside the system by virtue of the fact that I could be drafted but I couldn't vote.   *Tom*

Now, coming out of a civil rights movement that was all about voting rights, that was insupportable.   *Jane*

We had pamphlets that were aimed specifically at high school kids and the rights of high school kids. "You're about to be of age to be drafted into the Vietnam war but you can't vote!"   *Sue*

END OF STUDENT DEFERMENTS

The manpower needs of the war were ferocious.   *Bob*

Then we were aided greatly by General Lewis Hershey, who was head of the Selective Service, one of the great organizers of anti-war protest in American history because General Hershey announced that the draft would have to start taking students. People would be able to get deferments to the extent that their grades warranted it and therefore that students' grades and class standing were to be reported to their draft boards. Suddenly the American campuses became aware of the possibility that some of their number were going to be selected for this war.   *Dick*

All around us at the University of Texas we had friends being sent to that war. And it meant that the guy who was in your algebra class or your history class may six months later be drafted and sent to Vietnam — to kill or be killed.

Jeff

The notion that your performance in school would be decisive in whether you were going to end up face down in some jungle was, I think, quite horrifying and directly and profoundly affecting to quite a few people, including faculty like myself.

Dick

Universities were forwarding transcripts and class ranks to the Selective Service System. We demonstrated against complicity with the war.   *Bob*

We said: we will not submit our grades to the administration so long as the administration is determined to do these class rankings in cooperation with Selective Service.

We needed the students to back that and it was expressed in a sit-in, an occupation of the administration building, which was one of the first after the Berkeley Free Speech Movement. It lasted 4–5 days and there were 1000 or more students who occupied the administration building.   *Dick*

A bunch of us were eventually suspended. I lost my scholarship money for a semester.

Bob

DRAFT EXAM

In addition to grades, students had to take a test to help determine their draft status. SDS saw the occasion of the exam as a chance to reach thousands of students with a different message.

This was the ultimate high-stakes standardized test. If you did poorly on this one, you could come up as a high priority to be drafted and shipped to Vietnam.

Sue

We thought it was vicious of the government, in the first place, to ask guys to compete with one another, even intellectually, academically, over the question of who was going to get drafted and who was going to stand above the draft. And that was the government's idea — that those who scored poorly would be subject to the draft and if you were a smart kid you wouldn't have to go. That seemed just ridiculous, beyond immorality almost.

SDS folks decided that the way to respond was to generate a test of our own, on the theme: what do you know about Vietnam? What do you know about the Viet Cong? What do you know about the North? What's your sense of the history of that place? Does it mean anything at all to you or is it just a funny looking word in the newspapers that you sometimes glance at on the way to the comics? So we generated a beautiful test.   *Carl O*

A number of us wrote a 'counter-exam' in which instead of asking IQ type questions (Joe and Charlie are traveling towards each other in two different trains, and so on), we asked about Vietnam. What does it mean to say there's a 'free-fire zone'? That was one of the questions. It means a place where the Americans think it's legitimate to drop their bombs anywhere they please just to unload them before returning to base. Lots of questions of that sort. We consulted a lot of knowledgeable people about Vietnam to make it up

We printed a half-million of them — and we distributed them at 850 campuses.   *Todd*

On the day of the national draft exam, we had picket lines strung up around the examination halls where these tests were being given. Cornell is a big school, it had probably 30,000 students at that time, and it had a lot

of male students taking the test — and probably a hundred of us outside telling them not to. We also distributed the 'counter-examination' that the SDS National Office had published which was supposed to show people how little factual information we possessed about what was going on.   *Sue*

DRAFT BOARD SIT-INS

In Austin, we started to look at strategies and what could we do to bring attention to the issue — and we came up with the idea of a women's sit-in.
Judy

This was 1966, it was years before the women's movement really sprung onto the scene and defined a lot of actions as women's actions.   *Alice*

The idea was that women could say, "We are wives, we are mothers, we are girlfriends, we are sisters — and we do not want our men to die in a war that is unjust and is wrong."   *Judy*

We went down and showed up in the middle of this draft office, and they called the police. The police didn't want to arrest us so they kind of stepped over us and we just sat there for, I think, six hours.   *Alice*

Austin Draft Board, October 1965. Alice Embree on right.

There was a plan at the University of Michigan to have a large rally, a protest, and then those who wanted to would leave that rally and march to the draft board and try to stop the functioning of the draft board and subject ourselves to arrest. And my brother and I debated it and discussed it and tried to figure it out.

On October 15, 1965, we had a rally of several hundred students — and we were surrounded by several hundred who were opposed to what we were saying. When we marched to the draft board, we marched through the town and we were assaulted and shouted at and attacked by lots and lots of people. And when we were arrested, 39 of us, and carried to these police vans, we were surrounded by hundreds of jocks calling for us to be lynched.

Bill

David Bernstein being arrested at Ann Arbor Draft Board, October 1965

We went to court and we assumed we'd be slapped on the wrist. Many of us stood up and made statements. The judge was so enraged by all of us being so self-righteous that he gave us jail time.

Bill

end the war
INTERNATIONAL
DAYS OF
sds PROTEST sds
OCT. 15-16
in Vietnam

TAKING ON THE SELECTIVE SERVICE SYSTEM

The summer between my freshman and sophomore year I decided to work in an auto plant outside Detroit. We had spent every morning after we got off the night shift, Pat and I, deciding what were we going to do about it, this draft that was out to take us off and have us fight. And we decided that we just could not be drafted, we would not — that we would refuse to go fight in the army in Vietnam. And then the question became: well, how do we do that? If we feel that way, shouldn't we be trying to end the war that's trying to draft us? And we looked around and we said: there's this thing called Students for a Democratic Society, let's find out what it's about.

Mike

Mike Spiegel, 1964

We decided to take on Selective Service — and to try to wreak havoc with it.

Carl D

We went out to dozens of high schools and bombarded the kids with literature about the draft and avoiding the draft and non-cooperation with the draft — and where to go for information.

I went with a group of women into the Los Angeles Induction Center. We were dressed up and we walked in as though we were secretaries or something and then we went to the left with the guys lining up for their physicals — and found ourselves in a locker room full of guys lined up in their underpants. We gave them all flyers and by that time someone had come looking for us with the police and we had to climb out a window, which we did, on the street level — and we escaped and we didn't get arrested.   *Sue*

I got my draft notice in 1966 and I was to report for a physical examination at a center in Detroit. I'd gone through this with friends so I had an idea of how I wanted to do it — and the way I wanted to do it was to show up with hundreds of leaflets explaining who I was and what I was doing and my intention to refuse the draft even if I passed the physical, and encouraging other kids to do the same. Every station I went to in the examination, I tried to agitate and speak. I started to pass out the leaflets and they took the leaflets but I continued to speak out. At the end of the day I did actually flunk the physical — I tried very hard to flunk it and I did flunk it.   *Bill*

The message we were trying to send people about dealing with their draft boards was basically, "Fuck the system." The message we were trying to send people was: you don't have to respect this system, you don't have to obey its rules, you can take its rules and turn those rules upon the system itself — to bring it to a grinding halt. It's kind of like the old trade union strategy of 'working the rule.' When people had a contract dispute with an employer, the workers would say, "All right, we will follow our contract and we will follow your instructions, Mr. Supervisor, to the letter." Of course, the assembly line would come to a grinding halt and that was what we wanted to do to the draft board.   *Mark*

The opposition to the draft was serious — and many faced arrest and jail for their actions.

There were demonstrations where young men got up and burned their draft cards, which threw them in jeopardy of going to jail.   *Jane*

I felt a real responsibility in the movement for people who might otherwise become accidental victims. Here I am preaching: resist the draft — tell your draft board to take a hike, don't show up. Here I am telling people in the military: desert, or sabotage things. Well, you can't say that without thinking that you have a very real-world responsibility to help these people out when they get in a jam.   *Mark*

Cornell vs. THE DRAFT

Henry Balser,
Cornell SDS

The left at Cornell is getting serious. We are beginning to realize that, if we want to change this country, we are going to have to work hard and risk a lot. Right now, the idea of draft resistance is growing.

Five Cornell people started a national call for 500 or more people to burn their draft cards on April 15 at the Spring Mobilization in New York. The Mobilization is amenable to the idea, and important support has been received (Staughton Lynd, Paul Goodman, Dave Dellinger, et al). Finally, it was decided to solicit names at Cornell.

We ordinarily have a table at the "student" union to sell literature, publicize campaigns, etc. So the SDS desk was used to solicit names for the draft card burning. All went well for a while. Twenty people signed up. But then a student government committee decided that what we were doing was illegal and that we could not use the campus for such devious purposes.

We naturally decided that risking university disciplinary action meant nothing if some of us were risking five years in jail. The confrontation with the administration gained a lot of support, and at a rally in the student union, we talked about Vietnam. And we talked about a country where the university felt that it should enforce the Selective Service Act on campus. And people listened. We talked, without the rhetoric that we too often used, about being human beings in a country that is committing genocide. And now more than forty people have signed up to burn their draft cards if 500 others do. Many people who had never before participated in any form of civil disobedience have signed up. And 200 people sat in at the administration building to protest the actions taken against us.

And we are not just taking this action. We are going into the dorms, fraternities, sororities, and Ithaca High School talking about the war and the society out of which it grows. Our success in this has been amazing so far. For some reason, there is a growing sense of urgency about the war. Partially, this is because Stokely Carmichael came here and turned people on. And James Bevel came and people were thinking more about what they should do. Then came this confrontation with the draft system and the administration of Cornell. We expect that at least 50 people from Cornell will burn their draft cards if the required minimum of 500 is reached. And it could be even more on campus where one could not have expected to see more than fifteen or twenty do this.

We have been able to use the Mobilization as a tool in organizing people here. Those who have been adamantly opposed to the Spring Mobilization, as I and many others have been, should perhaps reconsider. Attendance now means support of those who are refusing the draft. And we are making it very clear that it is not a demonstration to end all demonstrations. We know that demonstrations will not end the war, but we can use them as a tool in involving people. When someone expresses his opposition to the war and a desire to go to New York for the march, he is told that his job is to get others involved and thinking. And an organization in which they can work to do this is being set up. We are not just getting the same old people.

The Mobilization, including the draft card burning and some of the other militant actions planned along with it, has given the movement a shot in the arm at Cornell. Literally hundreds are working on the draft card burning and the Spring Mobilization. We will continue to solicit names for this action in spite of any administration rules. Those of us whom the administration knows will be put up for disciplinary action, but others are refusing to give their names. They will have to arrest us, but they are afraid of that. The last time the cops came on campus was to confiscate the literary magazine for obscenity. 2000 people rioted. And now, with a pot-LSD bust going on, things with regard to the law are rather touchy. We are now essentially breaking university regulations and getting away with it.

We still need more people to join in the April 15 draft card destruction. This will be the first really massive form of such a serious kind of civil disobedience and draft resistance. For copies of the pledge, write to Bruce Dancis, 107 Dryden Road, Ithaca, N.Y. 14850. Sign up for civilian life.

New Left Notes, April 1967

SDSer gets 6 years

Bruce Dancis, Cornell SDS, was sentenced to six years on November 12 for ripping up his draft card in December 1966. Although he was tried in federal court for violation of the Selective Service Act, carrying a maximum sentence of five years, he was sentenced under the Youth Corrections Act, denied bail, handcuffed to two Federal marshalls, and hauled away to the maximum security cell block in Onondaga County Jail.

Sentencing under the Youth Corrections Act is possible for anyone under 26. Under the guise of protecting the young (the felony does not go on your record, thereby permitting you the privilege of voting or holding state office after your release), sentencing is for an indeterminate period of time. By imposing an indeterminate sentence of 0-6 years, there is the possibility of an early release if the prisoner "reforms". In political cases, it's clear what constitutes a "reformed" person.

Judge Edmond Port accused Dancis of inciting to riot and suggested that he begin his education in jail. As he was taken away, Dancis agreed that he would use the time to read all of Marx.

After a petition campaign to release Dancis on appeal bond got 5500 signatures at Cornell (1000 signatures obtained at the Cornell-Dartmouth football game), President Perkins of Cornell (on the Board of Chase Manhattan) telegraphed the court for Bruce's release. This Tuesday, the appellate court released him pending appeal. At an SDS rally to welcome him back to campus, Dancis denounced the tactivs of Perkins and attacked hus role in defense research and imperialism.

New Left Notes, November 1967

So one of the things that we set up was, in essence, an underground railroad, a way of getting people to Canada — safe houses where they could stay with people who we at least hoped were not under surveillance, and get IDs, access to jobs and transportation, and that sort of thing.   *Mark*

I was talking to a woman one day on campus who said a good friend of hers had gotten a very high lottery number which meant he was going to be drafted and sent to Vietnam and could I help him? So I met with this fellow.

There was a whole series of draft counseling information that you'd give to people. Here are your options: you might want to go to Canada, you might want to drop out and use an assumed name, you might want to stay in the country and continue this kind of work in another part of the country. You might go into the military and resist, you might go into the military and organize GIs.

People would examine their options. A good organizer never dictates to people. You say, "Here's the options," and you talk with them. He wanted to drop out and go to another part of the country so our concrete problem was getting him another set of IDs. You tried to use as many third parties as possible so that if somebody was a government agent it was hard for them to arrest you because, "All I did was give information." This guy goes to a place and gets this envelope, "Somebody left this envelope for you here." He actually went to another city and got very involved in the anti-draft movement there with a different name. He'd gone from being a-political to, "Gee, this is really serious, I have a duty to tell other people."   *Jeff*

Jeff Shero, 1966

People in a situation like the war years are confronted with deep personal and moral challenges. Because I'd worked in the underground press, I knew something about printing and got involved with an underground group of people who manufactured false identifications for people and helped them go underground or to Canada and other places. I had the bad luck of getting nabbed at the Houston airport — and they found 100 sets of false IDs for draft evaders.   *Jeff*

But we also kept a sense of humor.

For a while, there was no law against burning your draft card, there was only a law against not having a draft card. Well, people would write in to their board saying, "I lost my card." And now they had two cards, and they'd write in again and say, "I lost my card," and then they'd have three cards. And then somebody would stand up and burn their card at a rally and, of course, the FBI would show up at their house. "Let's see your draft card." And he'd take out his wallet and say, "You mean this," and light it right in front of them. And these FBI guys would just be seething and they'd say, "All right, you're under arrest." "What for?" "Not having a card." "Oh, you mean this." And out comes the third card. They'd go stomping off. You could just make these people apoplectic.   *Mark*

As time went on the draft became the biggest issue. No other issue could have divided men and women, I don't mean necessarily dividing them in a bad way, but women never faced the draft. No matter what we did, we were not going to get drafted, we were not going to go to Vietnam. And the men we were with — our lovers, brothers, sons — had to make decisions that we never had to make as women. I think one of the reasons the women's movement became important at that time was because there were issues, especially the issue of the draft, that so divided us.   *Carolyn*

7
Black Power

Many in the civil rights movement also joined in protesting the war — and SDS continued to work for civil rights. But tensions that had been slowly growing for several years within the civil rights movement came to the surface. Black power began to challenge the movement.

ROOTS OF BLACK POWER

We talked about making the decisions that affect your own life, and one of the things that was happening to blacks is that we weren't making the decisions that affected us — in fact, those decisions were being made by other people. I say that rather gently — sometimes it wasn't so gentle.

Carolyn

Race in the NCUP project [Newark Community Union Project] was the sleeper. The official SDS position was that race didn't matter — it was economics, it was class — so it didn't matter who was there organizing or where we were organizing. The poor people were supposed to get together and fight the system.

The people who were basically in charge were white — and they were from outside of the community. That became an issue, I won't say a problem — at first — but it became an issue to some people in the community because folks were saying, "Well, they're gonna leave one day and I'm still gonna be here."

That was what was happening in SNCC, in Mississippi and Alabama, and that's why SNCC said, "White folks, you gotta go." It wasn't meant in any other way, it was meant to say black folks at some point have to take the responsibility for their own destiny — and you, with your superior skills and knowing how to be articulate and having all of the social skills and graces that poor black people don't have, that became a significant issue.   *Junius*

I was working in Amite County in southwest Mississippi [in 1965] — where Emmett Till* had been killed. At that point the southern movement was undergoing a major shake-up. The back of segregation had been broken and the presence of large numbers of young white people the year before had really been instrumental in doing that, because it had brought a kind of political pressure and national consciousness to bear that — because we are a racist society, because we are a classist society — black folks in the South had been unable to achieve. And we'd done that. We'd been brought in to do that and it had, in very important ways, worked. Goodman and Schwerner getting killed — Chaney happened to be there, if it had just been him it wouldn't have gotten noticed — but those three boys getting killed really was the thing that opened it. That martyrdom was necessary.

So there were all these young white folks, all highly educated, all achievement-oriented, all kinds of access to resources and skills, with the unwitting arrogance of that privilege. And it was creating tremendous strains in the movement.

I became aware of it very concretely when I tried to organize a quilting coop. I was working with women in Amite County who'd been school teachers, some of whom had Master's degrees. I was 22 years old, these women were in their 50s, 60s, 70s. I knew they were smarter than I was, I knew they had it all over me. I was simply trying to facilitate the creation of this quilting coop to create a petty industry. And I couldn't get past the, "Yes Miss Jane," "No Miss Jane" — and people wouldn't come to meetings.

There was something going on among the group of women that I didn't understand, that I wasn't privy to, and I didn't have the smarts to figure it out. I could not overcome the fact that my skin was white. And in relation to these older people, that was an insurmountable barrier.   *Jane*

MARCHING THROUGH MISSISSIPPI

In May 1966, James Meredith, who in 1962 was the first black student to attend 'Ole Miss', the University of Mississippi, began a march for civil rights across Mississippi.

*Emmett Till was a 14 year old black boy from Chicago who was killed in 1955 while visiting relatives in Mississippi.

We heard on the radio that James Meredith had been shot in Mississippi. These guys were all upset about it, and I was too, and I said, "Well, let's go! Let's do it." We'd heard on the radio that other people were coming to finish his march. The two older black guys had an old beat-up Oldsmobile. I said, "Do you think it'll make it to Memphis?" They said they thought so. I got two other guys, there were five of us altogether, just on the spur of the moment, just like that. I got a friend of mine from the Philosophy Department to cover my classes for me, and we were off to Memphis.

When we got there, it was late at night and people were gathering at the church right next to the Lorraine Motel, the same one where King was killed later on. And we slept on the floor of the church and the next morning a bus took us to the Mississippi state line. People were already a few miles into Mississippi at that point and we started marching, walking through Mississippi. We were going to walk 250 miles, from the state line to Jackson. Some of my friends went back but I decided to do the whole thing and it turned out to be an experience that changed my life more than anything else.

I went down there wearing an army field jacket and an old straw hat and I had a Farmworkers Union button and an SDS button. I think I went into that march with somewhat radical non-violent Gandhian kind of politics and at the end I think I came out of it as a revolutionary. I spent about three and a half weeks altogether and got one of the best educations I ever had.

Every night we'd stop in these little towns, sleep on the ground in most cases. Sometimes they'd disperse us to different places — sometimes we'd sleep on a church floor, sometimes we'd stay in people's homes. When people would put us up in their homes, we'd get a feeling for the poverty, the utter poverty, of the people. I remember one little town named Batesville, where this one kid from Nebraska and I were invited into this sharecropper's home. Actually she was a schoolteacher and her husband was a sharecropper. They had us sleep on the bed and we said, "We don't really need to sleep on the bed, we can sleep on the couch." But they said, "No, no," and we had to sleep on the bed, which was a mattress on the floor. The next morning we found out that they were sleeping on the springs. But that's the way people were.

The husband took us into Batesville and as we drove into this little town he pointed out the security they'd set up. You could hardly notice it, but on this little porch, in a rocking chair, someone was sitting with a shotgun. Somewhere else there were a bunch of people sitting with their rifles. The whole place was armed self-defense, organized by a group called the

Deacons for Defense. This was challenging to me and I said, "What about Dr. King, he's supposed to believe in non-violence?" He said, "Dr. King should believe in non-violence, Dr. King's a man of the Gospel and that's what he's supposed to do. But we also have to take care of business. We support non-violence, we're completely non-violent unless people get violent with us — and we're here to make sure that the people like Dr. King can go out and preach non-violence." I know this wasn't supposed to make sense according to strict theory but in the reality of rural Mississippi it made a whole lot of sense. I was thoroughly impressed.

In Camden the local principal of the black school had decided to let us sleep on the school grounds, and the powers that be decided against it and they sent the State Police and all kinds of people out, armed to the teeth. They fired their shotguns up in the air and tear-gassed us — it was my first whiff of tear-gas — and people got whooped. I remember standing there as the police were coming. I started singing, "We shall not be moved." Stokely [Carmichael] came along and grabbed me by the scruff of the neck and said, "Get your ass down on the ground and stop singing because they're going to start shooting," which they did. Finally we got out of there and a black church took us in and we ended up in the basement.

The greatest lesson I learned in Mississippi — actually there were two great lessons — the first was the importance of class in reinforcing domination and white supremacy, because we could see up front how the structure of poverty and wealth were all tied in with the whole structure of white privilege and segregation. The other lesson that was very important to me was about black consciousness.

The Meredith march was where Stokely for the first time launched the slogan 'black power.' I remember one night we heard that Stokely was going to give a speech in a little church out in the middle of nowhere — one of these little clapboard churches, very poor. So I went, along with one other kid from Nebraska. We were the only whites there. The church was full, about 100-150 people, all sharecroppers, older people, younger people, kids.

Stokely came in and started giving a speech about how black was beautiful. He talked about how black people had a lot of culture, they weren't culturally deprived, that these were the terms of domination. And he said, "The next time your little daughters tell you they have 'bad hair' because their hair is nappy, tell your daughters that they're beautiful." The whole place was just electric with revolutionary consciousness — about the importance of power and that they didn't have political power. We were sitting there wide-eyed.

We saw the response of people. It was just the most natural revolutionary thing in the world, this 'black power, ' this concept that Stokely was launching on this march. We were a little taken aback when we saw later in *The New York Times* about how terrible was this dangerous concept of black power. To us it was absolutely fitting; it was very good.

It came home to me again in a little town, I think it was Greenville, Mississippi. We stopped and I was sitting on a stoop and a bunch of little kids came up, as they always did, and they started playing with my hair. I said, "Why are you guys playing with my hair?" and this little girl told me, "It's because you have such good hair." And I remembered Stokely's speech from the day before and the reality of it just hit me.   *Carl D*

I was very worried about the turn that the movement was taking. This was the first turn away from integration and towards a new form of black nationalism. My approach through all of these years had been one of coalition-building — that all of the main streams of the movement had to unite, essentially around common economic issues, and it seemed that year after year something came up that was side-tracking that. And the black power issues was certainly one of those side-tracks, it was another wedge now between the black student movement and the white student movement. So I was very disturbed and I think many people were.   *Steve*

GO ORGANIZE YOUR OWN KIND

SNCC asked white organizers to leave — and organize in their own communities. That had many repercussions.

I saw black nationalism beginning to happen and I thought it was a pretty good thing, I thought it was an essential part of throwing off that "Yes, Miss Jane; No, Miss Jane" kind of conditioning.

Jane

It was time for blacks to organize their own communities and for whites to organize their own communities.

Carolyn

My own thinking was changing. SNCC was changing. I had developed the photo project partly as a way of creating a technical skill for myself which would make me useful as a technical source for the movement, as a white person. The notion of simply being a white person in an interracial movement wasn't going to work any more because the movement's sense of itself was changing. In the course of this time I decided it would be more useful to begin to organize in the white community than to try to do this technical assistance stuff in the South. So I decided to go to Chicago to organize white women, welfare women.

Casey

I decided that the thing to do was take what SNCC folks said seriously and go and organize white people. That's what I needed to do — organize white people. So I went north with the idea that I was going to organize, probably against the war.

Jane

I wrote this paper that summed up the things I had learned. First I learned the importance of power and reaching out to our own constituencies — this was a lesson I brought back from Mississippi. I also learned about the universities' tight integration with the military-industrial complex. And I had all kinds of anarchist ideas about getting rid of authority structures and abolishing the grade system. I tried to bring all this together, along with the radical tradition from the Midwest — the Wobblies and all that — and I wrote this paper that presented the student movement in a different light. It saw the student movement not so much as an adjunct of the labor movement or that students should go out and become an interracial movement of the poor, but saw students as an insurgent constituency in their own right — and that they were part of the mosaic of organizations that would have to come together with their own interests and their own demands as a kind of critical force. I decided to call it *Toward a Student Syndicalist Movement*. We mimeographed 200 copies and went off to Clear Lake, Iowa, to the SDS convention. The next thing I knew, I was vice-president of SDS.   *Carl D*

When the turn happened to black power, I was living in a black community in Cleveland, as an organizer. It never felt personal to me — I know that it did to a lot of people. It was a challenge. And the challenge was the understanding that race is not a black problem, race is a white problem. And if it's a white problem, and if you're a good organizer, what are you doing in the black community organizing black people to repair the deficits of their lives; why don't you go to the white community, organizing them to get over it, to reject it, and to change it?   *Bill*

It was really time for me to work in the black community. I was more needed in the black community than in the white. I was just another organizer in the white community and it was really different in the black community.   *Carolyn*

When Stokely Carmichael said what to me seemed obvious, I think at first it was not said with any bitterness, I think it was said with a lot of love. I think it started off gently and I think it got really hard. A lot of whites resented it, they didn't want to go to their own communities — but that really is where they needed to go and where they needed to organize. And as time went on in the '60s and '70s, the call for black power became stronger and louder and more strident.   *Carolyn*

When the Newark riot came, the rebellion, in July 1967, that pulled the covers off of everything and everything became racially polarized. The NCUP [Newark Community Union Project] organizers weren't afraid because they had friends, we all had friends, in the neighborhood. So I don't think anyone was ever physically worried about being in harm's way — but it became impossible after that for them to function. So NCUP, for all practical purposes, by the end of 1967 was no more.   *Junius*

The riots were in the summer of 1967. It became the beginning on our part, the white organizers, of seeing that it was time to detach some and to begin to find other ways of being involved. I never felt 'kicked out' in any way, but I did feel it was time to move on. And that was very hard emotionally. At that time, Newark to me was the Clinton Hill neighborhood and Newark to me was black Newark. So it did feel a little bit like leaving home. It was hard.

A group of us moved into another neighborhood in Newark, which was the white working-class neighborhood known as Ironbound. A lot of what we were saying to each other, and other people were saying to us, was that if we really wanted to deal with issues of race we had to work with white people — and that as white people we should be working with white people. And so began another community organizing project that lasted another four to five years for me.   *Carol*

There wasn't much more for a guy like me to do in a ghetto. So I felt my part is to help end this war — and maybe someday we can get back to these problems that we've been working on since the early '60s.   *Tom*

The legacy of NCUP is that it was the first group to really force the issue of change on a city that so badly needed it. It was the first organization in that period to be on the cutting edge for poor black people in the city. NCUP got involved with folks that nobody wanted to see aroused. Nobody wanted to see those people in Clinton Hill aroused and angry and politicized. That was the legacy.

What NCUP set in motion was a leadership training for a significant number of black people to become a part of the political experience to follow. It probably was the best leadership training opportunity for politically aspirant blacks in Newark, bar none, over the last 30–40 years.   *Junius*

8
Freedom is Contagious — Women Rise Up

The challenge to organize in our own communities had many repercussions, one of which was that some women began to look more
closely at their roles — both in the society and in the movement.

Being a woman in the middle of these social movements was thoroughly
contradictory. It was impossible — and completely opened worlds.

Bernardine

WOMEN IN SDS — AND IN THE SOCIETY

I felt powerful in the movement, for the most part. I felt powerful in
SDS. I had a lot of prestige. If I had anything to say, people listened. I never
felt disempowered. It wasn't that. It was that there was something topsy-
turvy about things, so that I couldn't find my way to work there somehow.
Now I might identify that as a feminist critique, but at the time I didn't.

Casey

Being involved in the civil rights and anti-war movement really allowed
thousands of women to feel confident and purposeful in a way that led to a
sense of identity as women, not just as actors in someone else's drama.

Bernardine

Being a part of SDS was a tremendous opportunity. It played itself out
as an opportunity primarily in the context of the community organizing
side of SDS.

Cathy

Women were very important in SDS. They may not have had public roles in that they may not have been the 'president' or the author of the major papers because that was not something that women were 'allowed' to do. Yet the presence of women was fundamental to the success of a movement growing and developing because what the women did was all about relationships and creating that sense of community. They were the primary organizers because organizing is a relationship activity. So women were the ones who did the weaving back and forth.

They also brought to the debate and to the conversation a level of issues and concerns that were different than what the men would be bringing. The men were very much interested in the theoretical and the political history of an issue whereas the women were going: wait a minute, right now this mother can't feed her child, or this man over here can't vote. And there was that level of nitty-gritty practical living that the women would bring to the conversation, to the debates.

Sharon

Within the [Newark ERAP] project I felt very respected and there was a kind of camaraderie among both the men and the women that was very comfortable. I know now, and I knew soon after that, that it was subtler than that.

Carol

I drove up to the National Office and I went inside and introduced myself and said I'd been in the Swarthmore chapter of SDS and I was just passing through town and wanted to see what was happening. Greg Calvert was the national secretary at the time and he said, "Do you know how to write a complete sentence?" I said, "Yeah, I do, I think." And we talked for a while, for about 2-3 hours, about what had happened at Swarthmore and Chester [ERAP project] and what I'd been doing recently and he said, "Well, the editor of *New Left Notes* disappeared about a week ago and we haven't heard from him and we think he went to California. You want to edit *New Left Notes*? Can you stay?" So that's how I became editor of *New Left Notes* — on the basis of a two-hour conversation with a complete stranger.

Cathy

One of the realities of SDS, during the period I was involved with it, was that it really did reflect the larger social division of labor.

Jane

Women had been typing the leaflets and mimeographing the leaflets, and so much of that kind of work, without recognition, while the men took the more visible roles.   *Alice*

The intellectual debate side of SDS, in my experience, was always very male-dominated. When I was a freshman, I saw the posters for the Swarthmore Political Action Club [SPAC, the Swarthmore SDS group] and I went to some of the meetings but they were very dominated by very articulate, very competitive, fast-paced men. It was such a new world for me, I had never been exposed to the world of intellectual combat. It was a complete mystery to me what anybody was talking about — and as a result, fairly boring. So I didn't go back after my first few forays.   *Cathy*

They would go on and on and do all this intellectual performance for each other.   *Jane*

There were a lot of women involved in SDS, quite a few very strong women involved in SDS — women who were unafraid to speak up at meetings, take leadership roles — but a lot of women were intimidated by very verbal men.   *Alice*

It was a leadership style which, I think, came to some extent out of a background in an academic community where debate and intellectual prowess were important, and in a student government setting in which there was also a certain intellectual competition. I observed that style to be the way the group functioned in formal group settings. Informally some of that carried over but individually most people weren't at all like that.   *Casey*

Most of the skills I use today, I learned in SDS. However, there were those moments in SDS when the doors were really slammed right in your face. And it was particularly painful because this was the arena that was supposed to be different than that. And so the sense of betrayal and the sense of bitterness when that happened were deep and profound.   *Cathy*

SEX AND CASTE

The first piece of writing about women that I was involved with in the movement was a piece that was written at the time of the SNCC Waveland [Mississippi] conference in November 1964. At that time everyone in the organization was invited to write about anything that was on their mind. I had a house in Tougaloo, Mississippi, the Literacy House, where a number of women had ended up living. By this time we were all reading Beauvoir, we had all read Friedan. We were all talking about these issues all the time. When the invitation came to put out papers, working with a list of situations of inequality for women that Mary [King] remembers drafting, a group of us put some material around that and we put it out as a paper. So that was the first instance.   *Casey*

Casey Hayden, 1960

That grew out of this group's feeling it was time to come out, a kind of coming out as feminists to the rest of the organization, putting our thoughts out there for everybody. So that had a kind of bitter tone to it, that piece of writing, but it was never meant for public consumption. It was like jostling amongst ourselves. Later it became public and it's much quoted. But it didn't really have that much impact at the time. Whereas a paper which I drafted later and Mary [King] and I mailed out to SDS women was received and picked up and, hey, they ran with it.   *Casey*

"Sex and Caste," as it came to be called*, was mailed to a number of women in SDS and SNCC in the fall of 1965. It was later printed in the April 1966 issue of *Liberation* magazine and reached a much wider audience.

It seemed to me that the next step was for women to talk to each other.
    Casey

*"A Kind of Memo to a Number of Women in the Freedom Movement and the New Left" was the title when the long letter was first sent out.

> . . . the problems between men and women and the problems of women functioning in society are among the most basic that people face. *"Sex and Caste", 1965*

Freedom is contagious. One group of people wants to be liberated, everybody wants to be liberated. *Bob*

There was a paper that was passed around amongst the women — and it talked about how as women in SNCC they were fighting for civil rights, for other peoples' rights, and suddenly they realized that they were second-class citizens themselves. *Marilyn*

> There seem to be many parallels that can be drawn between the treatment of Negroes and treatment of women in our society as a whole. *"Sex and Caste"*

They called on the women in SDS to think about their own situation. And I was very moved by this paper. *Marilyn*

I think that was the first time I had ever read anything which really talked to me about gender relationships and gender politics — and it all made perfect sense to me. *Carol*

FIRST SDS WOMEN'S MEETING

Inspired by "Sex and Caste," which a few of the women had already received, some women met separately at the SDS National Council meeting held in Champaign-Urbana, Illinois, in December 1965.

It was very contentious. The fact that women wanted to meet separately was seen as quite hostile and very exclusionary. *Vivian*

We began discussing what it meant for us to be women in SDS and what it meant to be women in our own lives, in our own bodies, and our own vision for ourselves. It was probably the most inspiring moment of those years for me because it made me realize that my own experience as a human being was really important. And here I was thinking about the Vietnamese, or the welfare mothers, or blacks — and suddenly the old memories came flooding back to me of what had happened to me at Little League, what had happened to me when I wanted to be a doctor, how I had to explain to my grandfather why it was OK for a woman to go to college, and how even in graduate school it was so difficult to be a woman.   *Marilyn*

It was all the issues — a lot of the issues that we had run into as community organizers — the issues that women really care about: reproductive issues, health issues, child care, schools, employment issues. And we were beginning to see those as organizing issues — and issues that affected us as well as the people we were trying to organize.   *Vivian*

WOMEN'S GROUPS

I went back to Chicago and the first thing I remember doing was that I got a group of women together in my living room and we wanted to continue this conversation about every phase of our lives. What was it like to grow up? What was it like to go to school? What was it like to be dating? What was it like to be a human being in a female body? It was one of the most important political meetings of my life. One of the first consciousness groups started right there.   *Marilyn*

Marilyn Salzman Webb (center), Washington DC, 1968

We started a consciousness-raising group — and it was within the context of that group that I began to develop a deeper understanding of my own oppression and also began to think differently and see the world differently. I often say that period was like putting on a new set of glasses and suddenly seeing the same things I had always seen but seeing them differently.   *Carol*

Over the next years, these kinds of conversations continued in living rooms all across the country.

So the women do all the support jobs and the men do all the intellectual work, what's that about? What is it in our upbringing, what is it in our background, that creates that as a natural way to behave — both in the larger society and in the organization? Why does that happen?   *Jane*

Most of the time it was women who would be really active in our organizations, who would be strong, who would be clear, who were the organizers — but whenever somebody was to be elected as the head of something, it was always a man.   *Carol*

I don't think that consciousness about women's liberation really came full-fledged into my mind until about 1969–1970. And it's almost as though the whole cerebral map changed. I began to see things in the context of how women had been treated, and how men had leadership roles and related to the women as girlfriends. Suddenly seeing the world that way was very startling. There was resentment and bitterness, a lot of looking back and seeing things differently.   *Alice*

We were talking about women and a kind of structural analysis of the role of women and then we asked all the men to leave. And the women started talking — before that the guys had been talking and the women hadn't been talking. Suddenly all the women started to talk, reporting out experiences. It became very animated and everybody was participating. Then the guys came back in and everybody shut up. And we said: there it is, that's it! It was demonstrable, that women shut up in the presence of men. And it wasn't necessarily that men were consciously doing anything. They weren't intending to shut people up. But just as in the South I had shut up black folk, so men shut up women. It was a structural relationship: that was the key to my understanding of what was going on.

I also worked out of a belief that women were the only ones who could break that system, that men could have the best good will in the world but women had to change that system. And you could only do that, to some extent, separate from men, as that little demonstration showed. Women had to get together in their own groups, discover their own potency within those groups, be able and willing to take those risks, so that they could then move into the larger movement.   *Jane*

Jane Adams, 1965

My perspective at the time was: we have the space here to make things happen. Take it. Don't work through men, don't defer to men, don't be their cooks and secretaries. We have the opportunity here to change the world — grab it, let's do it.   *Jane*

INFLUENCE OF VIETNAMESE WOMEN

In 1967, Vietnamese from North Vietnam and the National Liberation Front in South Vietnam wanted to convene a conference with American peace activists.   *Vivian*

When I went to the anti-war conference in Bratislava [Slovakia], the Vietnamese women were talking about the role of women in their movement and about gender politics and about sexism — and it began to awaken in me an awareness of issues of gender.   *Carol*

The Vietnamese women called a meeting for women only. I had been to a women-only meeting once before in 1965 at an SDS convention — and this was the second all-women meeting I'd ever been to. The Vietnamese women were extremely sophisticated about the importance of women meeting together because of the things that we had in common, the interests that we had in common, that we could only talk about together.   *Vivian*

The Vietnamese women were talking about women's issues in a way that really got some of the American women — it certainly did for me — to think a little bit differently and to question things a little bit differently about the relationships of men and women in the movement and in the country.   *Carol*

I saw the notion that women were actually a political constituency that's worth organizing — and that, as a woman, it was something that I could do, that it was a particular skill and ability that I had. I saw that this was my constituency, and that women were extremely important politically and should not be overlooked as a power and as a moral force. And so the Vietnamese nurtured my sense of myself as an important organizer and helped me think of how I could reach other women.

It changed my life. I came back to the United States and I was a public speaker. I had never spoken in public; I had never been asked my opinion about anything. I had to speak publicly, I had to learn to do that. I had to learn how to demand respect, to organize my thoughts, to be effective — and it really changed who I was. It made a leader out of me.   *Vivian*

MEN

Being an anarchist, I was somewhat sympathetic to the women's position because to me — women's liberation, right! Abolish patriarchy, right on! Down with all authority! But I didn't really understand it in real feminist terms. To us, abolish patriarchy meant overthrow the fathers — it wasn't so much aimed at husbands!   *Carl D*

I didn't have a developed understanding of the oppression of women. I can still remember that it was in 1966 that I first heard the phrase 'male chauvinist' — and it came as a shock to me.

It was similar to the notion of democracy in our country and that black people were denied the right to vote. The idea that we lived in a democracy and that women didn't have the same rights as men and the same opportunities, as obvious as that is, was not something that I was aware of. I was a man; no one had ever said to me or brought up that it was a problem.

No one had ever talked about it. And suddenly the women in SDS were saying: it is a problem. There's something going on here that you're not aware of, Mike Spiegel — and you ought to be aware of it because it involves *you* being in the position of oppressing someone else and taking advantage of your position as a man to get certain things in life that you think come naturally to you, but in fact are denied to me. Hearing that was a troubling thing. It was very troubling in the sense that obviously they were right. But, on the other hand, what do I do about this? And that was very confusing to me.

Mike

I think it was a really tough time for a lot of the men is SDS because they felt challenged. Everything they had been, all their leadership roles, suddenly the women were saying: be quiet, we're going to define our own agenda. The men were having to let go of things.

Alice

WOMEN'S RESOLUTION — 1967

The women's issue came to the fore in the national organization at the 1967 national convention in Ann Arbor. A number of women wanted to speak to the entire organization, to a plenary session, when all the delegates from all the different chapters were there, on the subject of the women's movement and women's oppression.

Mike

A whole group of us got together and wrote a resolution that was a call for women's liberation and it used the parallel of colonialism and colonial relationship and of racism and the racial relationship to talk about women and to say that the same things happen.

Jane

The leadership of the organization, a lot of the people who were very influential — all men — in the organization, really opposed it and did not want them to be able to speak on it, opposed the idea that there was such an issue. And the women actually had to force their way onto the stage at a certain point to make themselves heard. They spoke out very courageously in the face of cat-calls and in the face of real opposition from a lot of the men in the organization.

Mike

It was really quite a wonderful and electrifying experience. It galvanized the collected body. It was controversial but it was interesting how people didn't quite seem to know how to grapple with it.

Jane

When the issue of women did begin to be debated openly within SDS we were able to fight our way in the door and have that debate and that discussion in SDS in an ongoing way, even though it was at times attacked by some men.

Cathy

I simply don't think that the men in SDS were ready to accept that there was such a thing as a women's issue and weren't ready to really fully support it. And as progressive as we were around the war in Vietnam, as much as we understood the civil rights issue, when it came to us, and our role in the organization as reflecting our roles in the society as a whole, we were simply not ready to do anything about it.

Mike

Some of the men were very defensive and said, "We don't do this." As I recollect, our response was, "This is a system. We aren't saying that you're bad guys, we're saying if you look at the reality around you this is what it looks like — and as an organization we have to address it." We tried to be very gentle with the guys and say, "You're not evil but this is the system — and we have to change it." And so the resolution passed.

Jane

They couldn't really raise the issue within SDS and then see SDS take it on the same way we had taken on the draft or the war in Vietnam or racial oppression or economic oppression or any of the other things that we felt were wrong in society. That one SDS was simply not capable of picking up and running with. And so the women had to go outside SDS to form an organization that could articulate that issue.

Mike

This happened to us in a way that it wouldn't have happened in any other arena in American society. The things we did in the movement were things that women were just not given the opportunity to do. So we were a group of women developing skills and abilities that we couldn't have developed anywhere else but in the movement, but then there was really no place for us to take it in the mixed left. So for me the women's movement became the arena in which I could take leadership and build the kind of organization I really believed in.

Vivian

For the women who went through that there was a lot more energy, they were discovering things. And there was a lot of exploration with women of new forms of doing things, in women's organizations. I returned to Texas in 1970 and got involved in the early women's movement in Austin.

Alice

A NATIONAL WOMEN'S MOVEMENT

Out of the small groups, a movement took shape.

We kind of put little pearls together, one at a time, of the stories of our lives and out of that grew not only Washington women's liberation, but an idea that we wanted to have a national movement. There was a sense that these groups now were happening after the 1965 Champaign-Urbana meeting. These groups had already been started everywhere.

We did the planning for the first national conference at a place called Sandy Springs, Maryland. After that we put together one of the first national conferences in Lake Villa, Illinois, for the following Thanksgiving, where we really kind of mapped out a philosophy and theory and how we were going to organize essentially what became the national women's movement.

The Lake Villa conference was women from all over — not only from the left, from SDS, but women from NOW [National Organization for Women], from different aspects of the women's movement who wouldn't necessarily come in contact with us — and it was large, large.   *Marilyn*

We began to focus, in late '68 and early '69, on what was the most important direction that we could go in. Was it developing the idea of women's oppression, which meant that we had to really separate ourselves out and talk about this issue and work only with each other as women? Or were we models of women for other women in what we called the 'mixed left' — working around Vietnam and draft resistance and power structure research and anti-imperialism and support for civil rights, where those were the critical issues and our job as women was to support each other so as many women as possible could be active and successful in those?

At the time, many of us saw that as an either/or strategy — and we began to develop this ferocious confrontation within our women's group, and a tremendous sense of personal vulnerability amongst us about which was the right way to go when, in retrospect, of course, both were absolutely essential.

Cathy

9

Movement for a Democratic Society

As some students were getting older and leaving colleges and universities, SDS began thinking about a broader movement for a democratic society.

The ERAP community organizing projects had been one response
but they were not sufficient — they didn't fit for everyone. A few
Movement for a Democratic Society (MDS) chapters formed but
the idea never took off.

RADICALS IN THE PROFESSIONS

The people who had been the first generation of SDS were, for the most
part, past the freedom of student life — and people began to think of
family and career. And all those institutions seemed so tied in with the
status quo that it seemed very difficult to function in your professional life
in accord with the values that you held.

So this 'Radicals in the Professions' was an endeavor to transition from
simply being a student and an activist to being a long-term agent of the revolutionary process. It was the first generations looking to their future. *Alan*

We formally and informally tried to think through a form of new left
organization for professions or communities.   *Bob*

There was a Radicals in the Professions conference in 1967 that pulled
together radical teachers, radical lawyers, radical city planners, radical social
workers, radical doctors — to have a conversation about what would be the
role of a movement doctor, a movement lawyer, a movement teacher. What

would people do, strategically and tactically, to contribute to the movement beyond the days of students?   *Bill*

There had to be a place for like-minded people who were critical and saw the professions' role as keeping people adjusted and in tune with the ideology of the status quo. There had to be a place for the insurgents to operate.

Alan

Radicals in the Professions

Newsletter ⚭

published by:
Radical Education Project
Ann Arbor, Michigan

VOL. I, NO. 5
MARCH, 1968

Beginning to Begin to Begin

MOVEMENT FOR A DEMOCRATIC SOCIETY

Bob Gottlieb and Marge Piercy

Radicals in the Professions

Newsletter ⚭

published by:
Radical Education Project
Ann Arbor, Michigan

VOL. I, NO. 2
DECEMBER, 1967

ORGANIZING IN THE HEART OF AMERICA

Rich Rothstein

I want to suggest that radical professionals, and in particular stable radical professional families, should consider living in the kinds of working class communities where organizations of consumer protest and development of viable alternatives can be a part of their radical work.

Living in such a community can be a natural and genuine experience for radical professionals. It does not imply the artificiality in life style that a move into a very poor white or black community involves; and without this artificiality, the role of 'organizer' merges easily with that of 'concerned citizen'. The radical professional will find that, without posturing, he is not so different from his neighbors. A most significant section of America lives in these so-

called 'lower middle class' communities, usually suburban communities -- here teachers, factory workers, lower-level civil servants, craftsmen, clerical workers, and family doctor dwell together.

Levittown, Long Island, would be one such community; in the Chicago area, names like Roseland, Gage Park, Maywood, and Schiller Park come to mind; Somerville, Mass., of Anaheim, Cal., are similar. These are not 'middle class' communities in the 'upper middle class' sense which the movement is used to scorning; neither are they so poverty-stricken that rent strikes of welfare demonstrations are appropriate. These are the communities that feed the junior college systems, that worry about school and property taxes (not out of contempt for education, but out of economic necessity), and that elected Johnson because Medicare was a solution to

(cont. on p. 17)

Now what did it mean: 'radicals in the professions'? It meant we weren't going to be students forever, so where were we going to be radicals, because we were going to be radicals forever.   *Bill*

So there was a sense that we'd form a radical caucus in history and in political economy and in law and in social work and so on. And those caucuses grew up all over the place.

In all the different professions, we had been lied to, deceived, information was distorted. The whole university curriculum had to be opened up and revised and subjected to criticism. And so the 'free universities' began in New York, and Ann Arbor, and Berkeley, and I don't know how many different places.   *Alan*

COUNTER-INSTITUTIONS

We also experimented with creating new institutions.

If the institutions of a society are unjust, unfair, racist, inadequate to serve the needs of the people, what you do is you create 'counter-institutions' that answer all those questions. You have your own food cooperative, your own schools, your own clinics, your own music, and your own culture — and these are counter to the mainstream.   *Bill*

Bill Ayers, Children's Community, Ann Arbor, 1966

The Children's Community was an alternative freedom or 'free' school that I ran for a couple years in Ann Arbor — a very exciting, energizing life space.

We wanted to do two things simultaneously. We wanted to educate our kids in a way that was full and whole and meaningful and decent — and we wanted to prepare them for a life of purpose and energy and engagement. We wanted to prepare them to not just accede to the world as it was but to change the world if necessary. That's what we wanted for our kids. But we also wanted to be a model of non-racist, non-sexist, non-competitive education and we wanted that model to have an insurgent quality — that is to affect the other schools.   *Bill*

Shire School, San Francisco, 1968

SHIRE GOALS

We don't have a formal statement of these but the following may give you some idea of what we want to do.

- To help the child understand his environment and how it influences him.
- To help him feel confident in his ability to influence his environment.
- To help him learn to use the tools which are useful in understanding and influencing his environment.
- To help the child feel reverence for life, this life, now.
- To help the child feel strong and important and whole in the world, the world of what is, the world of conflict and strife and love and music and sunrises and fear.
- To help him accept now, even though it's not all pleasant.
- To be open and receptive to the beautiful and spend time exulting it.
- To be open and receptive to the ugly and spend time fighting it.
- To help the child discover what has lasting value to him, whether it conforms to our values or not.
- To protect and nurture the uniqueness of each child, for that is his value to the world.

Shire School, San Francisco, 1968

It wasn't good enough that we were going to do it for 30 kids, we had to do it for all kids. That meant that I was active in the union, it meant I was active in the school board, it meant I was active in citizen's groups that were active in education — and always with the edge of trying to use the Children's Community as a model of a better way and then as a tactic of insurgency.

Those kinds of notions — do we build a counter-institution or do we change the dominant institution — that tension is not easily resolved theoretically; it's not easily resolved in practice.   *Bill*

There were a few underground newspapers popping up around the country in 1966. Thorne Dreyer came back from California with this idea that we could do a paper in Austin. It was collectively run.   *Alice*

We needed a way to counter the *Dallas Morning News*, the *Austin-American Statesman*, and the *Daily Texan*, the University of Texas paper. Maybe we'd call it *The Rag*.   *Robert*

We had created an atmosphere in just 3–4 years of a real activist, investigative, question-authority journalism. And *The Rag* went from being printed in the bedroom of a little hippie house to have a phenomenal impact on our campus. We were selling 10-15,000 copies. It drove the president of the university, who was president of the Democratic Party of Texas, nuts. It taught me that clear ideas, and correct ideas, are very, very powerful.   *Jeff*

We started *Off Our Backs* in 1969. We decided to start a national newspaper to deal with women's news. It was pretty revolutionary at the time. We thought we would have a paper whose point of view was what was important for women.   *Marilyn*

People think of newspapers as institutions. The *Rat*'s not any separate kind of institution, it's just another organizer's tool. The underground press challenged authority and questioned authority in an era when newspapers didn't do that.   *Jeff*

The underground newspapers became a big part of the connective tissue of the movement, spreading ideas from one place to another.   *Alice*

Journalism was changed. SDS people at the chapter level started alternative papers that really questioned the authorities in their cities. And that perspective of how journalism is conducted has now become a mainstream idea.   *Jeff*

THE COUNTER-CULTURE

The counter-culture was broader than alternative institutions. And SDS ideas on the counter-culture varied with place and time.

From rhythm and blues I got interested in jazz music and I started hanging out with other kids who were interested in jazz. Later I had Allen Ginsberg's *Howl* handed to me in an Aliquippa pool hall. I read it and was just enthralled. It was through these cultural kinds of rebellion that I first came to politics.   *Carl D*

People out of the plains and the South didn't see a separation between politics and culture — we thought they were the same things and we knew that at the grass-roots level SDS was growing because it was connected to the culture. Of course, people are smoking pot, people are doing psychedelics, people are grooving to acid-rock bands, people are wearing long hair — these were signs of the rebellion that was taking place.   *Jeff*

I entered the youth revolution, the cultural revolution that was going full steam on the Lower East Side. I thought that meant I'd left the movement but I don't believe that any more. I think that in a larger sense what was happening there was also the movement and that I was a bridge from one to the other.

The society's values were being torn off like old clothes and tossed to the wind, right and left. People gave away their belongings, they created art to their own standards, they made new musical forms, they moved to the country and experienced the fact of the dissolution of the ecological substructure of the planet. They rejected hypocrisy, they thumbed their nose at authority, they had babies, they studied Yoga, they transplanted Eastern philosophical thinking to this country. I did all of that.

I moved to the country and began to learn how to do organic gardening. I looked for community in all this and built community. Then I had kids, and had to support them. I chose a marginal life.   *Casey*

Texas wasn't an environment that was conducive to dissent!   *Alice*

If you can't go home and have your family reinforce you, your friends become your family — and in Texas our friends became our family because we couldn't go home to our families, many of us, most of us. So we lived together, ate together, went to jail together, protested together, worked together, made love together, took psychedelic drugs together, and danced together. We did it all. There were lots of tight bonds and it was a wonderful thing.   *Jeff*

The group coalesced as a social group, as a community. It wasn't like a political group that you join and you go to a few meetings or you pay your dues. This became a very significant thing in all of our lives. Our romantic lives were mingled with our political lives — it was all part of the same fabric.   *Alice*

In Texas SDS we were concretely challenged with relating to regular people and so we devised a tremendous number of campaigns that reached out. We teamed up with a lot of the bands and had a lot of political be-ins against the war. For example, in the local park by the library we had a big Vietnam protest that was basically a picnic, rock and roll bands, and political speeches.   *Jeff*

There were bands that we considered to be part of our community. The 13th Floor Elevator crowd was on the picket line — and we went and danced to the 13th Floor Elevators at night.   *Robert*

In 1965 we headed out to San Francisco where we set up the first SDS regional office west of the Mississippi and really started organizing on the West Coast. Not only did I come to San Francisco, but my first home was in the Haight-Ashbury. It was the beginning of the hippies, and there were thousands of them in the streets, there was music in the parks, there were plays in the parks.

Carolyn

Artist Wes Wilson made posters for anti-war rallies as well as rock concerts.

I arrived there in late 1966 and very, very shortly discovered the wonders of the burgeoning counter-culture.

The SDS regional office shared space at that time with the San Francisco Mime Troupe, which occasionally would lend its space to rock bands to practice in. So here we are trying to start a revolution and what ultimately became the Jefferson Airplane is firing up in the corner and cranking up its amplifiers.

Mark

We had this huge dance and got busted by the Fire Department — too many people came — and they threw us out and we had to give the money back to most people. A couple days later [Mime Troupe manager] Bill Graham came into the office and said he'd found a place to have another dance and that it was going to be at something called the Fillmore

Auditorium. This was a building that had been abandoned and empty forever, I think, and we thought he'd lost his mind. But sure enough we got it together and organized a dance at the Fillmore with the Jefferson Airplane, Big Brother and the Holding Company and Janis Joplin — everybody was going to sing. Five thousand people came and Bill Graham spent the entire evening wearing saddlebags draped on his shoulders with all the money that we had raised. The next day Bill Graham came into the office and he had two pieces of paper in his hand. One was his resignation as the manager of the Mime Troupe — and the other was a five-year lease on the Fillmore Auditorium. And the rest is history.   *Carolyn*

DRUGS

There were a lot of times when it was a lot more fun to just drop acid and listen than it was to get out another three boxes of leaflets.   *Mark*

I was against the drugs. I always thought that drugs had absolutely no part in this. I didn't believe in the psychedelic revolution, always thought that drugs made people crazy and subject them to arrest and diverted them off into odd thoughts.   *Steve*

We were always aware that we were under a lot of surveillance by the FBI and the LA Police Department. They were very open about it, they would photograph us coming in and out of meetings. So we tended, at least those of us who were organizers and in the leadership, to be pretty conservative in terms of the use of pot. It's so much an intrinsic part of the culture in Southern California, it's as casual as having a beer. It was not a casual matter for people on the staff of SDS because it put the reputation and resources of the organization at some risk. If someone at an SDS chapter meeting, for example, had pulled out a joint and started to pass it around, other people would have said he must be a cop and would have been suspicious.   *Sue*

We heard that somebody in our office had smoked dope and that was so serious that we fired them. That wasn't just because we were straight. We thought that what we were doing — as organizers against the war, as organizers around civil rights, as organizers around campus issues — that those issues were so important that we could not afford to be busted over something silly like smoking marijuana.   *Carolyn*

Marijuana was important because it was illegal. It was the fact that it was illegal that made it really important, because as soon as you smoked dope suddenly you were illegal, you were outside the law, you were an outlaw. And for a young person to be an outlaw is a pretty heady thing, that's fun. But I think the psychedelics were much more important in terms of creating a new consciousness.   *Jane*

In Texas and elsewhere, we ate peyote, which the American Indians did. We had a peyote-like Indian philosophy of the inter-connectedness of the universe, which was a whole precursor to the environmental idea.   *Jeff*

Psychedelics, more than grass, were really, really important to the nature of the movement that formed up, the youth culture that formed up, and those two being overlapping. Psychedelics provided access to an experience of what I call the sacred, of a radically altered state of consciousness that was not available through any other means to us. It was an experience of the world that was novel and unique.

It was part the burgeoning shift in trying to find new ways to look at the world and to understand the world. It was a way to find a spiritual dimension to the world.   *Jane*

This was one of the things that became, I think, a link between the organized left and what ultimately grew up to become the environmental movement. Hey, I was a city boy — I grew up in cities. I liked going for walks in the country but I didn't have any particular feel for it. I had no innate sense within me that I was somehow connected physically or organically to the rest of the universe.   *Mark*

One thing that came out of the experiencing of psychedelics was a new way of understanding the natural environment, because part of that state that you experienced through psychedelics was a continuity of self with the rest of the world, instead of the barrier. It's that a tree is as much a living entity in the world as I am. It's a really different way of understanding humans in relation to the world. And that, I think, has been profound.
                    Jane

I think the ecology movement comes out of the Vietnam War because people who saw what we did to Vietnam reacted to that. And those of us who went to the communes began to relate to natural ways of being with things — living with forests and with trees. You look at Vietnam and see the napalming of the trees. Napalm is supposed to be a defoliant, by the way, you're not to use it against people.   *Robert*

The experience of psychedelics gave us a powerful respect for non-Western ways of doing things. That's very important if we're ever going to have a diverse world where we really do permit and appreciate diversity. That's a key element of recognizing that there really are radically different ways of understanding reality — you're as much human as I am, even if you think really differently than I do. The psychedelic experience was a key part of opening that up.   *Jane*

I think in the long run the greatest ground-breaking we did will be the planetary spread of the notion of a holistic world-view. We penetrated Western dualism, we put a hole in the dike.   *Casey*

The problem was that at the same time that we were trying to make room in our lives for this sort of thing or, more accurately, at the same time that these kinds of experiences were pretty much kicking down our doors and demanding our attention and our focus, people were being burnt to death in Vietnam, people were getting shipped overseas and chopped up and coming back in bags. And we were trying to have this sense of being open to what was going on in the world and what was going on in the rest of our lives and at the same time there was this ongoing horror of being aware of what our country was doing to other people and trying so desperately to stop it.   *Mark*

LOOKING BACK

I thought that the counter-culture had a very destructive effect on SDS and I thought then, and it eventually turned out, that it could be totally co-opted into a new form of consumerism. And it brought with it attitudes and styles that were incompatible with making political change, among other things because a lot of the so-called counter-culture was aimed at a youthful sense of shocking and embarrassing adults, and so it set young people off from adults. But, of course, adults were the majority of the population who you needed to organize to make democracy work. So I thought it was a political disaster. However, here's the paradox that shows that my opinion is about something complicated. The paradox is that absent the counter-culture, the mass diffusion of resistance ideas, the enthusiasm of young people probably would not have been there. You would have had a smaller movement. So the choice was maybe a smaller and somewhat more rational movement or a really large totally incoherent movement. We got the latter.   *Bob*

But it also brought a sense of play into the politics that was so important. This was a terrific antidote to taking oneself too seriously.   *Mark*

I also think people who tripped a lot lost their hold on reality in important ways.   *Jane*

I spent an awful lot of time trying to talk people out of looking like hippies or being hippies. In the earlier days, whenever we had a picket line or a demonstration and somebody showed up with beads and sandals, that was always the person that the television focused on. They were trying to marginalize us. And consequently, throughout the whole New Left period I was always trying to get people to look and act as mainstream as they could. The only result of that was that everybody got mad at me.   *Steve*

There was something about the counter-culture that was entirely positive. It wasn't new with the counter-culture, it was old, but it needed bringing back. And that is: bread and roses. There's this great song that came out of the Lawrence strike of 1912, which was basically conducted and won by women textile workers. They carried signs that said, "We want bread — and roses too." The counter-culture reminded the world that apart from needing material things and more money, we needed beauty and community and hope and dignity. The counter-culture understood that.   *Bob*

Probably the thing I regret the most about my role in SDS was a fundamental misunderstanding about the nature of the youth culture and the movement that emerged in the mid-Sixties. I attributed a lot of it to political error. I thought that people had mistaken ideology and that was why they let their hair grow long and dressed funny. I didn't realize what the movement was, I didn't realize what a cultural phenomenon was.   *Steve*

I came to believe in the counter-culture as a social force when I got to Santa Barbara — I hadn't really seen it until I got there. There was this intense feeling of anger at authority, at constituted authority — and a belief, on the other hand, in their own creative potential. I think it was not just a negative resistance, there was a lot of amazing action and talk after these events, and a year after, about community building and trying to create some vision of a participatory democratic community right there in the student world.   *Dick*

10

The War Continues — Resistance

By 1967, most of us felt that the war had undermined our project of trying to recreate this interracial movement in the cities and in the South and Appalachia — and that it was really the war that had become our ultimate problem to confront.

Tom

We didn't experience the war as some blurry backdrop — and by the time when I was doing this work in the fall of 1967, the daily details of American strategy in Vietnam were as much a part of our life as getting up and brushing your teeth and drinking a cup of coffee. We knew the landscape of Vietnam, we knew the provinces, we knew the history. We had been in debates and arguments and by publicly speaking all the time we had to know, better than the State Department officials who we were debating, what the arguments were. And we did. So the body bags and the casualties and the failed military strategies and the constant lying from the State Department reports on the nightly news were very much a fabric of what was happening.

Bernardine

It was not just another war; it was a war from the horror chambers.

We — it hurts to say 'we' — were using weapons of extraordinary destructive potential against churches and schools and bridges on the grounds that somehow the economy of Vietnam had to be attacked, and the social-political infrastructures, in order to destroy the enemy's will to resist. The [Bertrand] Russell Tribunal on War Crimes was able to put its hands on a US Army manual that in no uncertain terms described the various kinds of targets and why each particular kind of target was necessary. It specifically named the morale of the other side's population as a legitimate military target, specifically said that the way to destroy the morale of these people was to hit them in such as way as to cause the maximum pain to the civilians.

We were using phosphor weapons, we were using cluster bomb units against them. The 'cluster bomb' was particularly insidious. There was a big 'mother bomb' that contained inside it smaller bombs that the Vietnamese called 'guavas.' The big bomb would get to a certain low altitude and then burst and the small bombs would be thrown out in a saucer pattern around it and these bombs were filled with little pellets. When those bombs blew up, the pellets would scatter all over the place like somewhat larger BBs. And the point was: they didn't kill people, they wounded people — and we wanted to wound them because this would overload their hospital system, which we knew was primitive. And by overloading the hospital system, we would destroy their morale, their will to resist. The theory was they would get more quickly tired of resisting us and give up. It was so painful to find out about these things.   *Carl O*

Poster by Jude Binder, 1965

It was just one scalding wound. You woke up every morning to new news of abominations, new evidence that the United States government didn't care a fig about what the American people thought. The US government hid behind every legalistic subterfuge imaginable in order to conceal from the American people what it was doing in Vietnam, and not only to the Vietnamese and the Laotians and the Cambodians, but also in a big way to the Americans. That was, I think, one of the staggering discoveries for a lot of us.

I mean, you can understand that the government had mistakenly embarked on a crusade that was, come to find out, foolish and unnecessary. But to think that the government would use weapons like the phosphor and the napalm and the guava bombs against civilian targets — and moreover hide this from the American people, as though it were secretly ashamed of what it was doing. This wasn't what the American government was supposed to be about — we were fighting in Vietnam to save those poor people for the free world. We supposedly were fighting for the great ideas of democracy and the republic. In fact, what we were doing was opposing those great ideas and undercutting our own moral standing in our own eyes.

Outside napalm factory near San Jose, California, 1966

With every can of napalm that got dropped, the American constitution died a little bit. With every village taken out, the Declaration of Independence became a little more meaningless, so that for the American people, the war in Vietnam became not just a crusade on behalf of others but a fight to save the guts, the core, of our own culture. We couldn't possible call ourselves a democracy-loving people and let that war in Vietnam go on. We had to do, finally, everything that could be done, at least to let the world know that there were some good Americans who wanted that crap to stop — and hopefully to go beyond that and make it harder for the war-mongers to do what they wanted to do.   *Carl O*

RESISTANCE

SDS's ideas of how to stop the war were changing. Instead of polite protest, people began to talk about resistance.

Our government is doing something in our name that is criminal, immoral, deadly. And what's happening in the course of us opposing it is ripping off everything we grew up believing: that democracy works, that a lying government will be found out, that sending young men off to subdue a country that is obviously not going to be occupied — and resisted occupation for 2000 years — was cruel.   *Bernardine*

Cathy Wilkerson, Washington DC, 1968

We protested for civil rights, we protested against the war, we protested. But then we began to realize that if we really thought those values were important, that they weren't going to come about in this society just by protesting.   *Cathy*

Most of us couldn't vote, we had no access to the levers of power. The democratic system couldn't work for us except by supplication, and clearly supplication wasn't working and petition wasn't working. And so the only way we could act was to resist. And then there was a moral dimension of resisting, witnessing, placing our bodies there.   *Jane*

It was at this point that we began saying: OK, if the cops throw tear gas at us, we're going to throw it back. If they're going to beat us, we're going to wrap newspapers around our arms and consider putting on football helmets so we can withstand that.   *Elizabeth*

So we were no longer appealing to the powers that be to do their job right. We were saying, "You're doing you're job wrong — and we're going to stop you."   *Jane*

From protest to resistance practically speaking meant that the SDS chapters increased their level of militancy. They also got more diverse in terms of the targets that they picked. One thing that was especially popular was that we did a lot of research investigating universities' connections with different aspects of what we called the 'war machine.'   *Carl D*

We thought that the universities were ivory towers of intellectual exploration and learning — and yet we came to find out that the universities were really arms of the government and that enormous amounts of research money was poured into the universities to research the war in Vietnam for the government, for the army.   *Cathy*

There was research by SDS members on every campus to find out about these kinds of connections. The Dow Chemical Company — which was the developer and manufacturer of napalm, the incendiary jelly that was the most horrific anti-personnel weapon — was a major endower of both Michigan State and the University of Michigan and had research contracts with both universities, with their physical chemistry departments.

This was shocking to people. You think your mild-mannered chemistry professor is just researching for the benefit of humankind? Well, maybe not.

Sue

Students were trying to make the connections between the war and their university as part of the war machine. That they had a ROTC program that was training prospective officers to take part in this or similar wars; that they had research contracts that were developing weapons systems and spy systems; that we were personally benefiting, or our institution was — all that needed to be exposed. The same people who were telling us to just study and stick to our lessons were heavily engaged in war-making.   *Sue*

So exploring and challenging the university to rise up to some moral standard was one major piece of what we did.   *Cathy*

I started out really with a sense that the war was wrong — and in the course of all these activities got exposed to a lot of ideas which started broadening my view of what the problems were.   *Elizabeth*

MCNAMARA AT HARVARD

In late 1966, Robert McNamara, who was then the Secretary of Defense and therefore the highest official in the Johnson administration in charge of the war in Vietnam, was invited to the Harvard campus to speak to a seminar on American policy. When we heard about this, that this man who was literally the person in charge of the war in Vietnam, was coming to our campus, well, first of all we were outraged at the whole idea that they would even talk to him. Second of all, we thought: if he's going to come, we want him to speak to everybody — and we want a chance to ask him questions. So we developed a campaign to have him debate Robert Scheer, the editor of *Ramparts*, a liberal/radical magazine [who was also visiting Harvard at that time]. McNamara would have none of it, Harvard would have none of it — but we built up quite a publicity campaign around it and it was a very reasonable demand. All we wanted him to do was to talk — explain his policies, subject his policies to questions in front of this campus, instead of being closeted away with 12 students.

He did come and he was scheduled to speak at Quincy House, which was one entire city block surrounded by an iron picket fence. They got him in there somehow.

We called a demonstration and we marched down to Quincy House and we spread out around Quincy House, chanting and carrying our posters saying, "Come out and talk." And Robert Scheer was there. We had a bullhorn.

We decided to try to confront him as he's leaving. There weren't enough to actually surround the entire city block, there were probably 800–1000 of us. So I was with a group of four or five who went over to one little side entrance. Other people were over at the main entrance. At one point they actually sent a decoy out of Quincy House. They had a garage door that suddenly opened up and a big black limousine drove out with a guy sitting in the back dressed to look like Robert McNamara. Everyone ran around to that area and tried to stop that car.

I had been placed at one of the back entrances and my job was to stay there so we didn't leave. While everyone had rushed around to where the limo was coming out of the garage, the four or five of us were left alone.

Suddenly down the walk comes Robert McNamara. In front of him are two guys the size of football tackles, huge guys, coming at us — obviously Secret Service agents or some kind of body guards — and there's Robert McNamara right behind them. They're coming at us so we linked arms with each other and the people on the end linked their arms around the iron picket fence — and we just stood there. Well, these two fellows broke through us like we were paper, it was nothing. At the same time a Harvard University security car, a station wagon, zoomed around the corner and pulled up right there and the door flies open for Robert McNamara to jump in the car, which he does.

I went around to the front of the car and just sat down. I didn't know what to do. And somebody else went around and sat down behind the car. I just grabbed on to the bumper. And I remember holding on to the bumper of this car and I'm looking over the hood of the car and I'm eyeball-to-eyeball with Robert McNamara. He's looking at me, I'm looking at him — and I'm holding on for dear life. He's not going anywhere. And I think I'm shouting, "Why won't you debate Robert Scheer?" Time stood still. I had no idea of what was going on around me, I was frightened to death. I was gripping that bumper with all my might and there were security guards who had me literally lifted off the ground, pulling at both of my arms trying to get me off the front of the car. And suddenly I realized they just weren't pulling on me anymore — and I was still sitting there. And I remember turning around and looking behind me and it was a sea of people, filling the street, all sitting down. Robert McNamara was caught — the car couldn't go anywhere. So we got Robert Scheer over and we got out our bullhorn and Robert McNamara got out of the car and agreed to get up on the roof of the car, the station wagon, and debate Robert Scheer right there on the spot. And we asked him questions.   *Mike*

Meanwhile, the security people had infiltrated on the other side of the car, a line of them, between the car and an entrance to another building, and at some point, when they had gotten themselves into position, one of them, right in the middle of something he was saying, reached up and grabbed Robert McNamara by the legs, lifted him up, and they passed him hand over hand, over their heads, into the building. There went Robert McNamara, sliding out of sight, hand over hand, with these security guards, into the building.

That was the last time that a cabinet member spoke outside of a military installation in the Johnson administration. From that point forward, Robert McNamara never set foot on a campus, never set foot in a public forum where people could actually face-to-face ask him questions. And it became a model for the Nixon administration which did the same thing, where they would only give speeches in settings that they could control with absolute military security. We had created a situation in which the leaders of our country were incapable, and frightened to death, of going out and actually speaking to the people who elected them.   *Mike*

DECEMBER 23, 1966   NEW LEFT NOTES   3

report from Havard

MacNamara Blows His Cool

by Jon Wiener

When Harvard announced that Secretary of Defense MacNamara would come to Cambridge as the first honorary fellow of the Kennedy Institute of Politics, Harvard-Radcliffe SDS began a campaign to get him to appear publicly to answer war critics. Since MacNamara was coming the same weekend as New Left candidate and Ramparts editor Bob Scheer, a debate was proposed. Richard Neustadt, head of the Institute, refused for MacNamara; SDS got 600 signatures on a petition demanding a debate. Neustadt again refused, saying MacNamara was being brought for "informal contact with the academic community." The issue thus became whether public officials had an obligation to face the public. SDS announced it would demonstrate outside Quincy House, where MacNamara was meeting with 50 students, and attempt to "physically confront" the Secretary when he left, asking him either to agree to debate Scheer or answer questions right there.

Initially, it was not clear whether SDSers would turn out in large numbers on Monday after a weekend that was to include appearances by New Left culture heroes Lyndon Johnson, W. C. Fields, Timothy Leary and Bob Scheer. But Monday the weather was good, and, in anticipation of a big demonstration, Quincy House patriots hung sheets out their windows bearing the slogans "Kill the Cong," "Back Mac," "Napalm SDS," and "Black Day for Garden Linen." Loudspeakers blared "Mack the Knife" across the courtyard.

By 4 p.m., close to a thousand demonstrators (The Crimson said 800) ringed Quincy House, covering virtually all the exits. SDS heads ran a James Bond-type operation, with walkie-talkie equipped spotters on all sides of the building. After several false alarms and one attempted decoy maneuver, MacNamara emerged in a police car on a narrow back street. While a dozen SDSers sat down around the car, others passed the signal over the walkie talkies around the block, and the thousand began running toward MacNamara. Within moments, he was surrounded by what must have looked to him like a mob of howling beatniks; they were actually normal Harvard people, including faculty like Michael Walzer, delighted to have trapped the Secretary.

The rest is now history, although the New York Times garbled it a bit. What MacNamara said was, "I spent four of the happiest years on the Berkeley campus doing some of the same things you're doing here. But there was one important difference: I was both tougher and more courteous." After laughter and shouts, he shouted vehemently. "I was tougher then and I'm tougher now!"

The audience loved it. Mac was blowing his cool — unable to handle himself, quite possibly scared. The first question was about the origins of the Vietnamese war. "It started in '54-'55 when a million North Vietnamese flooded into South Vietnam," Macnamara said. "Goin' home!" someone shouted. Mac countered "why don't you guys get up here since you seem to know all the answers?"

The next question asked for the number of civilian casualties in the South. "We don't know," Mac said. "Why not? Don't you care?" came the shouts. "The number of casualties..." Mac began, but was drowned out by cries of "Civilian! Civilian! Napalm victims!" A few PL-types in front were jumping up and down screaming "Murderer! Fascist!" Mac tried to regain his composure and said "Look fellas, we had an agreement . . ." A girl shrieked "What about your agreement to hold elections in 1956?"

Things seemed to be breaking up. The police moved in and whisked MacNamara into Leverett House; an SDS leader, fearing violence in the streets, took the microphone and ordered all SDS people to clear the area. The disciplined shock troops of the revolution turned and dispersed quickly, MacNamara was hustled out through steam tunnels, and everyone went home to watch themselves on TV.

Official Harvard was unhappy. MacNamara's "I'm tougher" remark made all the 6 o'clock news broadcasts and the TV films looked violent. Deans were "appalled" and "amazed that students at Harvard would use tactics like this." Neustadt said that MacNamara had no obligation to answer SDS questions — "I see no reason why an educational experience should be changed just to suit someone else's convenience. It's like saying to me I should change the curriculum of my course because students don't think it makes sense."

SDS leaders replied to the Deans by emphasizing the alternatives they had proposed — speech, debate, petition. "When a public official reneges on a responsibility, and when all other avenues are closed, it becomes necessary to do what we did," one said. SDS noted that MacNamara was never in physical danger, that the TV films had been edited to give the impression of maximum chaos, and that MacNamara hadn't helped by taunting the crowd.

Finally, official Harvard apoligized, and an SDS head commented, "We had a feeling that the war was slipping back from people's thoughts . . . Now, everybody's arguing, and that's just the way it should be."

from the Dis-Center
Princeton SDS

MORE ORGANIZING — MORE RESISTANCE

We started out having very small debates on the war on the steps of the main library [at the University of Maryland]. They had very big imposing stairs where people used to congregate. We would have arguments about the pros and cons of the war — and people would gather around. It would become these huge kind of soapbox debates where people would get very involved in talking about how they felt about the war. And after an hour or two of this we would pass a sign-up sheet or a notice of a meeting saying: there's going to be a meeting to talk about this more — anybody who wants to come, come to the Student Center or wherever. And people would come and we'd talk about SDS and the various projects that SDS was working on.   *Cathy*

There was a dedication to debate and discussion, this belief that you can change people's minds if you engage them in debate and discussion. So one of the things that we used to do a lot of was we'd go door-to-door in the dormitories [at Columbia University] and have meetings on a particular floor on a particular night for anyone who'd want to discuss what it was that SDS was involved in. Sometimes there were five people, sometimes there were fifteen, sometimes there'd be very conservative jocks or engineering students, who were always considered the most conservative. And we'd get involved in incredible discussions.   *Juan*

Resistance took many forms.

I was trying to figure out how to do military organizing. This was a big issue for me personally because I was just about to turn 18 and I was going to have to register for the draft.

If we were really going to build a movement to end the war, that movement had to involve people who were already in it — because they were waking up in Okinawa or Subic Bay in the Philippines or in Vietnam the same way we were waking up in Berkeley or Austin, Texas, or Denver, Colorado. The wake-up call had gone out to all of us pretty much at the same time.

One of the principals that moved our anti-draft work was that even with the people we could not keep out of the draft, we were sowing the seeds of resistance, we were laying the groundwork for an opposition that would be within the military. People from all over central and northern California would get funneled through the Oakland Induction Center on their way to the army, the marines, etc. This was a place where we regularly did organizing. We'd show up 5:30-6:00 in the morning when people were lining up outside and we'd be passing out anti-war leaflets, giving people advice about how to get out of the draft if they wanted to get out of the draft, explaining to them how they could contact us.   *Mark*

When ROTC would set up to recruit we'd go and argue with them — and, at a certain point, we would turn over the tables, we would throw the literature on the floor. This was very confrontational because these guys were just everyday guys — this was not the head of the Pentagon behind these ROTC tables, it was some poor kid who was sent out to recruit on campus. So militancy was not an abstract thing, it was very much dealing one-on-one with another person and challenging somebody's work and their life.   *Cathy*

At Cal State LA they had these trailers set up where different corporations and branches of the military would send scouts to interview interested seniors for potential jobs. So when the Dow Chemical recruiter would come to the campus we'd get a couple hundred people and rock the trailer off its cinderblock foundations and turn it over.   *Sue*

We found a supply of theatrical blood — this is fine red powder that's dried blood, for use in movie sets. We'd take this to the induction center and we'd sprinkle it all over the floor. When you go in for your induction exams you have to strip down, so people are walking around in their bare feet. Next thing you know the floor is covered with bloody red footprints, which is quite appropriate. They'd get some janitor to come in and take a mop and put some water on the floor to clean it up — and it would turn into a river of blood.   *Carl D*

Los Angeles was a big transshipment point for weapons and for troops. Right off the campus of San Fernando Valley State College there was a US Air National Guard base which was being used to load bombers for runs to Vietnam. They actually saw the munitions on the runways. And so on several occasions, in 1966, '67, '68, bands of SDS guys would scale the fence, which was just a chain-link fence, you could actually climb over it. There was an orange orchard on one side — and there were bombs on the other side. You could climb the fence and lie down on the runway and block the planes from taking off, which takes a certain amount of nerve!

They would get arrested a lot, they got assaulted a lot, they got stuff thrown at them, they got beaten up. And then we'd have these wonderful parties to raise the bail money and to build support for this kind of organizing. It would always make the headlines, it would always make the nightly news. You'd see these blond kids lying down on the runways and going limp and being dragged off by four or five MPs and being thrown into the paddy wagons. It was quite dramatic.   *Sue*

Mike Klonsky arrested at Van Nuys (California) Air National Guard base, 1966

In all these activities, we often worked with other groups, including Stop the Draft Week in the San Francisco Bay area, mobilizing all SDS chapters in the area.

As resistance got bolder, the government reaction became more violent.

STOP THE DRAFT WEEK — OCTOBER 1967

A group based around *The Movement* newspaper in San Francisco began to have discussions about how to move the anti-war movement to the next level, whatever that next level was going to be, we didn't know. Part of this was that the war was going on, the machine was continuing to kill people, and we felt we had to do more.   *Mark*

In Oakland, California, immediately south of Berkeley, was a major induction center. And what we hit on was the idea of a week-long series of demonstrations aimed at blockading the Oakland Induction Center. We decided we would call this 'Stop the Draft Week.'

The pacifist slogan, and the individualist slogan at the time, had been: Hell No, We Won't Go. That was the individual standing up for his rights about the war. We tweaked that just a bit because we wanted to show what this was really about in our eyes. We tweaked that to: Hell No, Nobody Goes! We're shutting the Oakland Induction Center down — we're going to make this war machine stop.   *Mark*

STOP THE DRAFT WEEK
RALLY
PROVO PARK
Grove & Allston Way
Berkeley
OCTOBER 16, 7:30 PM

DON DUNCAN
Ex-Green Beret
JEFF SEGAL
National SDS Anti-Draft
JOHN GERASSI
Political Affairs, S.F. State

JOIN STOP THE DRAFT WEEK:
Oakland, 6 AM October 17

We have thousands of people converging from a couple of different directions on the Induction Center — and we're looking for the cops. It's dark, it's like 4:30 or 5:00 in the morning, and we're looking for the cops. We're getting to within a couple of blocks of the Induction Center and we're looking for the cops. Where are the cops? There are no cops. This is really weird. We get right butt-up against the Induction Center and there are still no police.   *Mark*

As we got to the Induction Center, I decided to go into the parking lot across the street where the press cars were and joined a friend who was with NBC.

At first the demonstration was peaceful but I could see what the demonstrators couldn't see — I could see Alameda County Sheriff's Deputies, as well as the Oakland Police, and I could tell they were ready for a fight because they had their batons out, and there was no reason for doing that unless they planned on using them. It was a very ominous and frightening sight. I knew there was going to be violence.   *Carolyn*

Oakland, California, October 1967

We get there and out from this parking lot and from a couple of other structures come pouring hundreds of helmeted and batoned police. We had not been prepared at all for this strategically. The first initial reaction was: everybody sit down. This will be civil disobedience, we'll sit there, they'll have to haul us away one at a time, there are thousands of us, this will take forever. Well, the police weren't interested in hauling anybody away — and the clubs began flying and people were getting beaten bloody instantly.

Mark

As the demonstrators got closer to the Induction Center, the police attacked them — and I think that was a real police attack, it had not been started by the demonstrators, the police were raring for a fight. As that happened, a lot of demonstrators ran into the parking lot where I was. I jumped into my friend's NBC car, which was clearly labeled an NBC car, and I locked the doors because I did not want to get hit by the police. The next thing I knew, my car was surrounded by Alameda County Sheriffs saying, "Nigger, get out!" They were beating the windows with batons and it was frightening.   *Carolyn*

Knowing there was going to be another demonstration on the Friday of that week, I said, "I've got to be there." We get there early, there's that sort of romantic dawn experience. There are thousands of us. There are apparently hundreds or thousands of police there. Lots of people who had been through the earlier demonstration had showed up with helmets.

When the police attack or try to take back various streets, the demonstrators have devised what they called 'mobile tactics.' The cops are coming down this street, so you dart around this corner and then you come back the other way. They are moving planters, big planters with big beautiful plants, into the middle of the street. They're moving cars, blocking the street. *Todd*

Oakland, California, October 1967

This was the beginning of our thinking that a small, highly mobile group of people reacting swiftly could be as effective or more effective in dealing with things. It was the beginning of what on the West Coast became known as affinity groups, collectives of people.

On that day, we actually did shut the Oakland Induction Center down. It was closed. Nobody had a physical, nobody was drafted, nobody got within blocks of the building. And this was after the police had already declared their intention and determination to keep this place open and functioning and to keep the war machine going, no matter what it took. The fact that we had beaten them at this was tremendously empowering. And it provided a tremendous amount of fuel and impetus for a lot of what was to follow.   *Mark*

Seven people — the Oakland Seven — including Jeff Segal, SDS's national draft coordinator, would later be indicted for criminal conspiracy as a result of Stop the Draft Week. After a long trial, they were acquitted.

TO THE PENTAGON — OCTOBER 21, 1967

The day after the demonstration at the Oakland Induction Center there was a huge national demonstration against the war in Washington, DC.

What came to be known as the Pentagon demonstration grew out of a large national mobilization organized by the Mobilization Against the War in Vietnam (MOBE), an umbrella organization of all the different anti-war organizations in the country. That year, the Pentagon had become a focus of the mobilization.

I was invited to give a speech there. It was the first time I ever spoke to a quarter-million people, it was kind of an impressive event for me. When I got up there I gave this militant speech focusing on draft resistance — I basically told people to disrupt induction centers around the country.   *Carl D*

We started at the Washington Monument and then we marched across one of the bridges into Virginia where the Pentagon was. And at some point, just after we had crossed the bridge from Washington into Virginia, a break-away group ran off and simply trampled down a cyclone fence.   *Mike*

We were right behind them and ran at full speed — and I guess most of the demonstration followed afterwards — across the field, over this little hill and up the back steps of the Pentagon.   *Cathy*

Outside the Pentagon, October 21, 1967

Outside the Pentagon, October 21, 1967

When you're in a large demonstration, it's not like watching it on television, you don't actually know what's happening in the front of the demonstration. In a way you're of it and in another way you hear about it later.   *Bernardine*

So here we were, 250,000 people, all outside the Pentagon — with thousands of soldiers.   *Carl D*

We charged up and literally ran up to the points of these soldiers with these bayonets. And there was a very, very tense moment because these were loaded guns and these were 18 and 19-year old terrified soldiers.   *Cathy*

I remember the troops being so terribly young and scared and trembling, holding these fixed bayonets but trembling. It wasn't like we were distant from them, we were intermingled with them.   *Bernardine*

Nobody was going anywhere. The soldiers weren't going to move and we weren't going to move either.   *Carl D*

And then we just settled in There was a certain amount of pushing and shoving and people putting themselves right up against the sharp points of the bayonets, taunting the soldiers.   *Cathy*

I don't think anyone had any real notion of what we were going to do. We were simply there to declare, right at the front door of the war-making machine, that we were opposing the policy in Vietnam — we were against the war and against the draft.   *Mike*

In my mind these war-makers were all inside peering out.   *Bernardine*

The Pentagon people had managed to present us with a couple thousand soldiers that we could sit there and rap to all day long about the war. *Carl D*

There would be long periods where they would simply be lined up face-to-face with us — and we would be sitting literally on their boots, right on their toes, at their feet. And we would be talking to them — and saying,

"Do you know why you're doing this? Do you know why you might be sent to Vietnam tomorrow? Do you know why you're being asked to kill people 12,000 miles away? Do you know what the point of this is?" We were attempting to raise the same questions in their minds that had been raised in ours.   *Mike*

Some of the soldiers tried to keep a very correct military posture and ignore us and look off into the distance, others sort of smiled and were somewhat sympathetic and got into long conversations. It helped a lot of us re-think and re-emphasize the importance of working with the military later on.   *Carl D*

WE'RE NOT AGAINST
THE SOLDIERS,
WE'RE AGAINST THE WAR!

Huge banner at demonstration, October 21, 1967

I think we came away from that with a new attitude towards work among the military.

Carl D

The soldiers weren't my enemy, it was the people who were sending them to that horrible duty in Vietnam.

Jeff

There was always a lot of conflict in our feelings towards the actual soldiers who went to Vietnam because on the one hand they were us. We could be drafted. We knew people who were drafted. Boys that I grew up with in Portland, Oregon, came home in pine-wood boxes. Friends of mine that I had played in the dirt with when I was a kid, were killed in Vietnam before they reached the age of twenty. And this young man who I was standing in front of the Pentagon addressing could have been my childhood friend. And I wanted, deeply wanted, to prevent him from being killed.

On the other hand, they were killing people, human beings also. We were always addressing them with a double message — and it was inherent in the position of being a soldier — that we identify with you, we empathize with you, you're going over to do something that could get you killed — but you're also killing other people. That's wrong!

Mike

We found out that a lot of the troops were shaken because they themselves had questions about the war.

Carl D

When we were in front of the Pentagon we were face-to-face with those young men and we were sending them both messages. You could probably see clips on television of us calling them 'pigs' — and you could see us sticking flowers in the barrel of their gun, saying, "Come with us. You don't have to do this. You can leave, you can go to Canada. Here's an anti-draft leaflet that explains to you how you can get out of the army."

Mike

Some of the soldiers listened — others used their clubs and bayonets on the demonstrators.

There were both the MPs, who were military personnel, who maybe had been drafted themselves but were simply young men, and there were US Marshals. They were brutal — they carried long night sticks and were beating heads. They were there to push us out of the way.

Mike

And then I remember bonfires and it getting dark and singing and chanting and begging the troops to come into the demonstration lines and a sense of euphoria, and a sense, that endless sense really of 1967, '68, '69, that the collective power of people actually could overcome technological and military might.

Bernardine

Outside the Pentagon

Many of us stayed all night. We all expected to be arrested, there was this tension in the air. I think they came out and told us we were going to be charged with a fairly serious crime and spend years in prison if we didn't leave. At about dawn they began to arrest people. It was a very anti-climactic end to it. They were very quiet arrests and many people walked away back through the short-cut and no attempt was made to come after them. So it was a very funny ending to this night.

It was a very powerful experience to actually be at the Pentagon, a few hundred feet from the 'war room' and the place where McNamara and others were making these decisions about the lives of the Vietnamese people.

Cathy

11
1968

When people talk about the Sixties, they're thinking of 1968. *Mike*

1968 is right out of a Francis Ford Coppola movie — it really was *Apocalypse Now*. That was among the most emotionally disturbing twelve months that you can imagine. *Bob*

That year went by in a rush of events that is like nothing that I've ever experienced since. *Mike*

1968 was a turning point in American life, and international life, and a whole generation, I think, never understood the world again the way that we had grown up understanding it. And when you look back at what happened in the first nine months of 1968, you can see why. World events were developing at a frenetic, an incredible pace. *Bernardine*

> On January 5th, 1968, Dr. Benjamin Spock and four others were indicted for conspiracy to aid, abet, and counsel young men to resist the draft. *Bernardine Dohrn, SDS reunion, 1988*

TET OFFENSIVE

> On January 30th, the 'Tet offensive' began when the United States Embassy was taken by the NLF [National Liberation Front] and held for a day and a night, with simultaneous military uprisings in 36 cities. *Bernardine Dohrn, SDS reunion, 1988*

The US generals in Vietnam kept saying, "There's light at the end of the tunnel. We're almost there. Just a little more money, a little bit more personnel — and we're going to have them beat." In 1968, at Tet, the Vietnamese New Year, the light at the end of the tunnel turned out to be a freight train coming in the other direction — the Viet Cong Express.

The Viet Cong attacked the majority of cities in Vietnam all at one time — and totally ended the idea that this was just a little insurrection, it showed that it was just a lie. This was a major insurrection. The Vietnamese people were fighting for the control of their own homeland — against us.

Robert

We had been told every night, "The body counts are going up, we're winning this war, we need a few more troops, that's all, just a few more troops. They're fighting with bamboo sticks, how are they going to defeat our B-52s?" And suddenly they had launched a coordinated attack all over this really large country.   *Mike*

For me to realize that the government was lying, cold-heartedly lying, not just a mistake, but lying on a massive scale, I think that's what got me.

Bernardine

> On January 21st and continuing for the next 77 days, until April of 1968, the Vietnamese military forces surrounded American military outposts on a ridge at Khe Sanh. During the siege of Khe Sanh, the United States dropped 220 million tons of bombs on the immediate surrounding area. It was the most heavily bombed target in the history of warfare.
>
> The drama and suffering of GIs during the siege ended with the United States abandoning the post at Khe Sanh in April. Khe Sanh stands for the willingness of the US to saturation-bomb Vietnam and to sacrifice soldiers needlessly.   *Bernardine Dohrn, SDS reunion, 1988*

PUBLIC OPINION

American support for the war was never the same after the Tet offensive.

Robert

In the course of 1968, as the Tet offensive refutes the government claims about how successful the war is, many people who had supported, or at least tolerated, the war start falling off the train — and they make a huge dent on public opinion. And they also send reverberations through the White House. Not least among them is Walter Cronkite, who gets up out of his chair, goes to Vietnam, looks around, comes back, gives a special broadcast in which he says: we should be seeking an honorable way out.   *Todd*

So when Walter Cronkite went to Vietnam and came back saying this is wrong, it was electrifying. Walter Cronkite! There is no more responsible person in the country than [CBS news anchor] Walter Cronkite. That was a tremendous change point. He created a space where all kinds of other people who had privately felt the war was bad could come out publicly.   *Jane*

The media finally stopped cheering the troops on and started asking questions.   *Tom*

San Francisco, 1969

And along with many other statements by respectable journalists, business people, professionals — doctors, lawyers, you name it — more and more respectable opinion is turning against the war.   *Todd*

On March 16, we now know — although it took a year and a half to unravel — several hundred children, old men and women were massacred in the village of My Lai. It took until November 13th, 1969, for that story to be reported by Seymour Hersh in *The New York Times*.   *Bernardine Dohrn, SDS reunion, 1988*

On March 12, Senator Eugene McCarthy won over 40% of the votes in the New Hampshire primary on a platform of ending the war. In mid-March, Senator Robert Kennedy announced he would be a candidate for president.

Then on March 31st, President Johnson went on television to announce he would not seek a second term.

I was sitting on the floor watching television in Newark when he resigned and I did a back-flip. I think it's the last time I've done a back-flip. This all had happened in a three month period, this was unbelievable.   *Tom*

And there was a sense of giddiness on the part of many of us that we had driven a president from office, again an unprecedented event, we felt, and it felt like we were gaining in momentum and strength.   *Bill*

We know now that LBJ's advisors had met with him that week — a group he called the 'wise men' that he convened from outside government periodically — and that their review of the briefing materials convinced them, a group of corporate and military leaders, that the United States could not win in Vietnam.   *Bernardine*

MARTIN LUTHER KING KILLED

There was a feeling that the left in the United States was surging and that the peace forces, the anti-war forces, the anti-racism forces, would come together in a majority coalition somehow behind Robert Kennedy, with the blessing of Martin Luther King. And then, bang, bang . . .   *Carl O*

Martin Luther King, murdered; then Robert Kennedy, murdered.   *Tom*

> On April 4, 1968, Martin Luther King was assassinated in Memphis. There followed uprisings by the black communities in 125 cities nationwide. 55,000 federal troops and National Guard units were sent to cities such as Washington and Chicago By the end of that single week there were some 46 dead and 20,000 black people arrested.   *Bernardine Dohrn, SDS reunion, 1988*

The killing of King was just enormously powerful because King had been this symbol of pacifism — and certainly militancy and forward motion —

but also pacifism and love and community. And King took positions then, on the war and against the war, and on poverty and against poverty, and named the system. Just like the progression in SDS, from protest to resistance, King was there. And from resistance to naming the system. And from naming the system, who knows. And suddenly King is gone.   *Bill*

In the week after Martin Luther King was killed, there were riots in 125 cities in the United States. I think it was probably the week that was closest to total civil disorder in modern American history.   *Juan*

Robert Pardun, Carl Davidson, Mike Spiegel, SDS convention, 1968

The National Office was in Chicago, just inside what was then called the West Side ghetto, the black community of Chicago.   *Mike*

I remember very well sitting on the roof of the SDS office watching the fires on the West Side and watching as the tanks rolled out of the West Side Armory.   *Sue*

The first night, because I knew it was on television, I thought I should call my mother. I was 20 years old and my mother, I knew, would be concerned that I was in Chicago and had no idea where I was, so I wanted to reassure her that I was just fine. I remember calling my mother in Portland, Oregon, and telling her I was just fine, it was no problem.

And as I'm speaking to her on the phone, there's a tank — which was right outside our office, and the turret of which was eye-level with me on the second floor of the building. And the turret suddenly started to turn around — and the gun on the end of the tank is aimed right at the window I'm standing in, looking out onto the street, as I'm assuring mom that everything is OK. I frankly did not think everything was OK — I thought it was quite likely that they were going to blow our office to smithereens.

Mike

During the riots in Chicago, after King was killed, Mayor Daley came on television and said the police will shoot to maim looters and shoot to kill arsonists. This is a shocking thing to say as a policy. A group of us had a demonstration downtown against Daley's outrageous statement and we were beaten to a pulp by the Chicago Police. This was a demonstration led by pacifists, there was absolutely nothing untoward going on — and they clubbed us and threw tear-gas and the whole business.   *Bob*

COLUMBIA UNIVERSITY STRIKE

Two weeks after that, on April 23, students at Columbia University rebelled.

There were three separate streams that brought the Columbia strike to the level and the power that it was — and they all came together on April 23rd.

The university was in the process of building a new gymnasium and they wanted to do it in Morningside Park, which was a public park adjacent to the university. So the black and Latino leaders in the area saw the gym as the final straw of years of university expansion and condemning of their land.

SDS was also conducting their protest against ROTC and against the Institute for Defense Analysis (IDA) and the research that it was doing for the Vietnam War.

So this is now a protest called by SDS against the suspension of a bunch of its members and against the Vietnam war — and everybody goes to this protest. All the black students go to the protest, all of us who are involved in the community battles against the gymnasium, everyone goes to the same protest. And there are thousands of people.   *Juan*

Everyone starts marching towards Low Library, which was the adminis- tration office, where a bunch of security guards push people back and it's clear we're not going to get into that building. Someone yells, "Let's go to the gym." So everyone marches several blocks over to the gym site and a bunch of people start tearing down the fence of the construction area. The police chase us back to the campus and we all end up in Hamilton Hall, the main student undergraduate building — and we began a sit-in there.   *Juan*

Columbia gym site, April 1968

Late that night a smaller group headed for the university president's office.

Early in the morning, about 2:00 o'clock, a whole number of people, maybe 50–60 in number, just broke through the dottering old guard who is sitting there guarding the building and stormed into Grayson Kirk's office and seized the office.   *Jeff*

Columbia University, April 1968

If you have never been involved in one of these take-overs, you really don't understand the tremendous elation that comes over a person when they break all the rules and create new ones. They sort of became little liberated territories.   *Juan*

In that office were files that proved every allegation about the university's connection to the Defense Department, to the various government agencies, and to the whole corporate structure that it was promoting and doing research for.

We were surrounded on the outside of the building by police and I packed all these papers together in a thick file and tied them shut and Frisbee'd them over the policemen's heads. Alice went to catch them and the corner of it caught her eye and she got a great big black eye, but she grabbed the papers and took off down the street and the police couldn't catch her — and we had the documents.   *Jeff*

There were a lot of documents from Grayson Kirk's office that pointed to all the connections — and these were things we knew about in the abstract. We knew that the Board of Trustees sat on the boards of major corporations and that they were involved in foundations that were funded by the CIA and that they were all part of an elite that was very much a part of how foreign policy was being played out. And we knew that they had links to real estate that was taking property all around the Morningside Heights area, that there were linkages to defense industries and defense contractors. But here in this briefcase was the actual evidence of that. It was proof that these connections really did take place in the way that we thought they took place.

I went through to see what was in there and then got them to the *RAT* office and went through to figure out what should go in the newspaper.

Alice

We printed a lot of these documents, proving our assertions, in the *RAT* newspaper. That was part of the power of the alternative press. The *RAT* did things that *The New York Times* couldn't or wouldn't do.   *Jeff*

So those documents made it into the *RAT* newspaper. And reference to them also made it into a document called *Who Rules Columbia* that was put out by NACLA, the North American Congress on Latin America, which was sort of a movement think tank doing a lot of research on corporations, on corporate interests in Latin America, on who the people were who were actually making foreign policy. With the strike at Columbia, some of that research began to really look at the connections the universities had with the war effort — with defense contractors and with all kinds of research that was going on, weapons research. These were some of the big issues at Columbia — and then they became issues at a number of other universities.   *Alice*

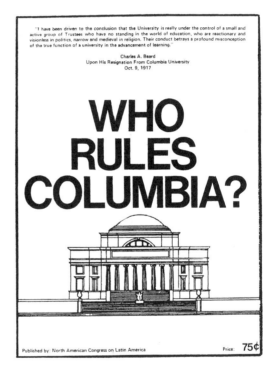

In one day, or a few hours, we had actually forced the whole university to confront what it was doing as a social force in American society.

Over the next few days several other buildings were taken until there were maybe five buildings occupied. I'd say there were maybe 1000–1200 students who were in and out of all of the buildings. We formed a campus-wide coordinating committee to become a sort of delegate assembly of all the buildings that then tried to decide the policy of the strike.

They sent hundreds and hundreds of cops the night of April 30th to arrest everybody. When the police came, there were a lot of faculty and students who got in between — trying to block the coming of the police — and many of them were beaten pretty badly. It was a pretty rude awakening for the whole campus. Over 700 people were arrested that night and I think 150 were beaten so badly that the police just left them in the streets.   *Juan*

Columbia University, April 1968

As a result of the arrests, we called a strike of the whole university and we must have had, within a few days, 10-12,000 people, of the 17,000 in the university, stop attending classes. And the university was shut down for the rest of the year. No classes were ever held for the remaining five weeks.   *Juan*

> Up until this time there wasn't a real radical movement, there was a movement of the mouth — and now there's a real movement in the sense of people committed to social change.
>
> *Juan Gonzalez, 1968*

It ended up: Grayson Kirk was fired; David Truman, the dean, was fired; the gymnasium was never built in the spot where it was supposed to be built; and we did stop the war research. So actually we won every demand, and we got all the people who had implemented the bad policies out. But we didn't see it that way at the time because they didn't actually do it when we wanted them to do it.   *Juan*

Juan Gonzalez, 1968

I was the first person in my family ever to go to college. So when I was suspended two weeks before my graduation, it was heart-breaking to my mother — my father had already died — and to everyone in my family.

Juan

TWO, THREE, MANY COLUMBIAS

Columbia wasn't the only campus facing angry students.

This was the height of the student movement at that time. SDS was growing so rapidly that we couldn't keep up with it.   *Mike*

At that point we estimated something in the neighborhood of 100,000–150,000 people who would have called themselves active members. On an average day, the National Office got two or three sacks of mail.   *Sue*

I was literally receiving phone calls several times a day from chapters that were new and that were calling the National Office to say, "Well, we got 250 people at a meeting last night, what do we do now?"

The National Office was in Chicago. It was the organization's center — calls would come in from the chapters, literature was printed and distributed from there, the organization's newspaper, *New Left Notes*, was put together, printed there, and sent out to the chapters. It was a place that a new chapter could call and feel that they were in touch with a national organization. It was absolute chaos. But we always welcomed people, in fact they would sleep there. People would come in from the local chapters to get a sense of the national organization, to work in the office for a few weeks, or months, or some people would stay for a year. The staff lived in one apartment on the other side of the block. We were paid the magnificent salary of $15 a week, which was our spending money since food and lodging came with the job. You had a place to stay, peanut butter sandwiches to eat, and $15 to spend as you will.   *Mike*

A group of us in Ohio and Michigan decided we'd start a regional office. There seemed to be a clamoring, it seemed to be a time when the movement was spreading way faster than the organizational capacity to keep up with that movement.   *Bill*

Part of what was wonderful about the Washington DC region was that there was a full-time staff. We all lived together in one house, to start with, of about 13-14 people. We all had little part-time jobs but I think the rent for this 9-bedroom house was $250 a month so each person only had to pay $25-30 in rent, and we figured out our meals collectively.

As the region matured, the SDS office was in a building with a variety of other organizations, like Washington Newsreel; Liberation News Service; Resistance, that was very active around draft resistance and the war and pacifism; the *Washington Free Press*, which was a major underground newspaper like the other underground newspapers of the time; we had our own print shop and print shop collective that was very active; and then by 1968 Washington women's liberation began to organize and develop.   *Cathy*

STRIKE FOR THE EIGHT
DEMANDS STRIKE BE
CAUSE YOU HATE COPS
STRIKE BECAUSE YOUR
ROOMMATE WAS CLUBBED
STRIKE TO STOP EXPANSION
STRIKE TO SEIZE CONTROL
OF YOUR LIFE STRIKE TO
BECOME MORE HUMAN STR
IKE TO RETURN PAINE HALL
SCHOLARSHIPS STRIKE BE
CAUSE THERE'S NO POETRY
IN YOUR LECTURES
STRIKE BECAUSE CLASSES
ARE A BORE STRIKE FOR
POWER STRIKE TO SMASH THE
CORPORATION STRIKE TO MAKE
YOURSELF FREE STRIKE TO
ABOLISH ROTC STRIKE BECAUSE
THEY ARE TRYING TO SQUEEZE
THE LIFE OUT OF YOU STRIKE

Posters from Harvard strike, 1969

ROBERT F. KENNEDY KILLED

On June 6, Robert Kennedy was assassinated in Los Angeles at his victory party the night of the California primary.

Literally Robert Kennedy was murdered at the moment that he'd won the California primary and might have been on his way to Chicago to win the nomination.

It was a cliché that it was the assassination of hope, but it was quite correct. I had very little hope left. It made some people go away. It threw all of us into a great quandary as to how the war could be ended. It was devastating — and for me I think it caused a hardening.   *Tom*

DEMOCRATIC CONVENTION — AUGUST 1968

In August, 1968, the Democratic Convention was held in Chicago.

1968 was also an election year and LBJ had stepped down and decided not to run again for president, clearly because of the war in Vietnam. Hubert Humphrey was going to run in his stead. Hubert had been his vice-president all through the prosecution of the war in Vietnam, and supported it throughout. And we were very single-mindedly focused on the war in Vietnam and opposed the election of anyone who had supported it.   *Mike*

The new goal was to put pressure on the Democrats to show that unless they really did something about Vietnam, they could not take anyone's vote for granted and they could not even be sure that they would have a complacent convention.   *Tom*

So we came to the Democratic National Convention in Chicago that year, August 1968, intent on showing that we were opposed to the war in Vietnam and we were opposed to the people who had pursued that policy. That meant being opposed to Hubert Humphrey. To some extent, many of the people who came supported Eugene McCarthy, who was really running on an outright peace platform. I think those of us in SDS were less concerned about Eugene McCarthy and the electoral political scene than some of the people who came. We were more concerned with the underlying policy and making it clear that there was a large and growing segment of the American people who were opposed to American policy in Vietnam.   *Mike*

I see it as being like an eruption of everything that had happened for the previous eight years. All the forces of the Sixties on all sides seemed to erupt to act out their identity on the streets of Chicago which, because it was a convention, also became a media event that was broadcast to the whole world.   *Tom*

I don't know why I went to Chicago except with the instinct of the moth to the flame. It was terrifying.   *Todd*

Chicago, August 1968

Right from the minute we arrived the police were aggressively pursuing us. Our car was stopped not ten minutes after we were inside the city limits of Chicago. We had out-of state plates and we were a Volkswagen bus with long-haired kids in it. Obviously we were there for the demonstration — and they were going to harass us.   *Mike*

I had been working for the McCarthy campaign in New Jersey so a group of us, two or three of us, went. It turned out that the McCarthy people couldn't use any more volunteers so we just joined the demonstrations along with everybody else. It was like being under siege. Row after row of jeeps with the barbed wire in front of them, the smell of tear-gas. You really felt you were in the middle of the most dramatic military situation.

We were running across the street, me and a good friend, Penny Chaloupka, and the cops grab her for no good reason. The guy goes to club her — grabs her hair and goes to club her. Penny is wearing a wig, the wig comes off, the guy clubs the wig, Penny scoots away. I don't know why she was wearing a wig but it was one of the luckiest things. That kind of random violence by the police was very much what was going on.   *Steve*

At one point, I was running through a street and a reporter for *Life Magazine*, who'd interviewed me some months earlier, suddenly appeared next to me, threw the car door open, and said, "Jump in." I sped off with him because he could see I was about to have the living daylights kicked out of me by the police officers.

And this was before the big demonstration which people now know as 'the whole world was watching' — the night of the nomination.   *Mike*

There was the big rally at Grant Park, at the bandshell. We were marshals, wore white armbands, helped organize crowds. We were around the outside, keeping order around the edges.   *Jane*

At that time I weighed about 154 pounds and I became Tom's bodyguard for Wednesday night and we went to Grant Park for the speeches.   *Bob*

A rally had started and there were people on the stage and they were proclaiming and strumming guitars. There were actually some people like Mickey Flacks who had been fool enough to believe in the democratic process and bring her child in a carriage. There were people who thought that nothing would go wrong because it had been announced that this was a permitted rally.   *Tom*

There was a very frightening moment when it looked like the crowd was going to be rushed by baton-swinging police. Allen Ginsburg was on the platform and he starts going, "OMMM . . ." — and everybody calmed down.   *Bob*

We noticed the police forming up in flying wedges and things started getting really electric. So we quickly formed a line between the police and the rest of the folks.   *Jane*

The police, as if on order, just started into the crowd. And Rennie [Davis], who is about as nonviolent as it gets and is dressed as Mr. Straight and has these marshals who are supposed to keep the peace, is saying, "Calm down everyone, calm down." And the police calmed him down — in fact they knocked him unconscious. I thought he was dead — they split his head. You know, a head wound causes massive amounts of blood. And all of a sudden there are all the people like Mickey Flacks with her baby in the carriage being gassed, things are being turned upside down, and we're right back to kind of a fist-fight, bedlam.   *Tom*

Chicago, August 1968

There was no provocation — the cops just decided they were going to clear Grant Park, and Lord only knows why. There was no outward reason, there was nothing we were doing, it was a peaceful demonstration — it was a fully peaceful demonstration. Nobody got rowdy until the cops started provoking us, and even then we stopped the provocations. We were clearly disciplined, we clearly had the crowd under control. Nothing was going to happen. They decided that they were going to clear the park. And they didn't even warn us, as I recall. Maybe they said we had to leave and everybody said, "Why?" I don't remember the whole sequence of events but the next thing we know they're lobbing tear gas and doing these flying wedges and smashing people and we're trying to keep order and take care of people and protect people — and it's chaos, it's just utter chaos.   *Jane*

I was quite hysterical because I didn't know how Rennie was. He had to be taken away by people in disguise into a hospital where a doctor in secrecy operated on him. He wasn't checked in under his name.

I got really into the moment and I started saying, "If there's going to be blood, let it be all over the street and not just here, and if there's going to be gas, let it be all over the stinking city and not on our heads right here. Take to the streets, don't get trapped in this park — I'll see you."   *Tom*

We were trying to help people get out. The way Grant Park is organized is that you go over the sunken railroad tracks to get out, and there are bridges only so often. Every block, I guess, there's a bridge to get out. So it's really a very difficult place to get out of. And we became aware that they were sealing off those bridges. They're telling us to clear the park and they're sealing us off? What are they going to do? And we had visions of them taking guns and just mowing everybody down. I mean, it was believable after the way they'd been behaving. Something very strange was going on.   *Jane*

They sent in these vehicles that we called 'Daley dozers' which were jeeps with big concertina barbed wire on the front rolling at you with guys in masks having a great time firing tear gas canisters. The effect of tear-gas is interesting. It's an immediate knock-out for most people. So we had to prepare to cover our faces with rags. It really looked eerie because of the lights of the jeeps, the tear gas going off creating this haze, and everyone running around with their faces covered. The effect of it, of course, was complete chaos.   *Tom*

Chicago, August 1968

So we started pushing people out of the park saying, "Get out of here, get out of here." And I remember, because those of us who were marshals were so busy getting everybody else out, we didn't notice that our avenues of escape were getting closed off. Suddenly the place is practically empty and virtually all of the bridges are sealed off. So we scurried down and we found one that was open. I have no idea to this day what in the world those cops were doing — but it was insane.   *Jane*

The park was filled with tear gas and I had to run through a lot of this gas to try to get out of there. I got over the one open bridge and I stopped at a water fountain to daub my eyes with water. I look up and there's another guy there and it turns out to be Jules Feiffer, the cartoonist, who had been an early hero of mine, who was there as a delegate for McCarthy. I introduced myself and we started running together, literally running down Michigan Avenue.   *Todd*

About seven bridges up, before you get to the museum, there's an open bridge — and everyone goes, "Hosanna," and runs over the bridge, before they cover it with the machine guns. So all of a sudden thousands of people have arrived on Michigan Avenue and now want to head back to the Conrad Hilton Hotel, which is about a mile the other way. Now it's starting to get dusk.·

And it got even weirder. Apparitions that I never believed would be seen started to show up. There was Ralph Abernathy with a mule-train of sharecroppers because way back in the beginning of 1968, which seemed millions of years before, Dr. King had wanted to have a 'Poor People's March' that would go to Washington and would come to Chicago perhaps. We had negotiated this and he had given his word. And now he was dead — but he kept his word. And there was this wagonload of sharecroppers from Mississippi and Alabama who were coming down the street, followed by what must have been five or ten thousand people.   *Tom*

At one point when we were in the downtown area around the hotels, the police decided to set up barricades and to push us out of the streets and onto the sidewalks. And they had these police barricades set up so we were really jammed in like sardines on the sidewalks, up against the buildings that were there. And then, out of nowhere, they tossed a tear-gas canister into the middle of the crowd that I was in. It was panic. People were knocking each other over and coughing and gasping and trying to move out of the way — but there was nowhere to go, there was literally nowhere to go. We were hemmed in on all sides by barricades and police. At that point people were really frightened and panicked.   *Mike*

People were getting clubbed. They had us up against the wall of the Hilton and they were clubbing people. We were so squeezed in tight, this was just vicious. A man on my left shoulder passed out and he was being held up by the bodies packed in there. I just thought we were going to buy it right there.   *Bob*

I was standing next to a window in front of one of the hotels and it was a display window. It had some kind of pictures or something and a little red velvet curtain and it was maybe a display window a foot or two deep. And next to me was a young fellow who was wearing a helmet. Now people were wearing helmets because there had been three or four days of these demonstrations and people had seen the police bashing heads, really bashing heads. I wasn't wearing a helmet because I was thinking a helmet would attract a police club and I was trying not to, so I didn't have one on. But I grabbed this fellow's helmet, I said, "Give me the helmet," and I started smashing out the glass of the window in the hopes that we might be able to go through the window and get out of the way because there was just no other exit.

Haymarket Bar, Hilton Hotel, Chicago, August 1968

So I broke the glass out and I jumped up into the window and I parted the curtain, having no idea what was on the other side of this curtain. I looked through — and I'm standing in a bar, behind the bar. There's bottles stacked up sort of step fashion behind the bar, there's a bar in front of me, and there's a dance floor. And over in one corner there's a band — and the band is playing 'Moon River.' And people are dancing, or they were dancing up until they saw me come through the back of the bar. And suddenly there's this guy lunging over the bottles. I knocked the bottles over, I stepped onto the bar. I can still remember this fellow sitting there with his drink, God knows what he thought was happening. And I jumped out onto the dance floor.

People started streaming through the window, tear-gas started coming through the window, the band stopped playing, people were in a complete panic. Then the police, who had entered the hotel through the lobby, came into the bar and were grabbing people that they thought didn't belong there — long hairs and people wearing jeans and so on — and beat them up, just were clubbing people, right in front of the patrons of the Hilton bar, the Haymarket Bar it was called.

I saw what the police were doing and stepped over to one of the booths and sat down next to a couple of young women who turned out to be delegates for the McCarthy delegation from Iowa, schoolteachers. I sat down and said to one of them, "Give me your beer and let's pretend we're boyfriend/girlfriend. You can see what's happening here: they're beating us up and if they realize I'm one of the people who came through the window they'll drag me out." And they protected me. The police were literally dragging people out from under tables. Eventually the police left with everybody they had arrested and these two young women escorted me upstairs to the McCarthy delegation and I watched that whole evening of 'the whole world is watching' on television with the McCarthy delegation.

The McCarthy delegates were outraged. They were extremely upset by what they were seeing. These were the Young Democrats who were working within the system and they were seeing what their own system was doing to people who protested. They were seeing it up close. I had an opportunity to talk with them about why we were there and what we were doing and why we had come to Chicago, because they had some misgivings about whether there should have been demonstrations in the first place because they were supporting McCarthy.   *Mike*

While outside...

The cops waded in and they started laying people's heads open — these kids in their suits and their dresses, they could have been fraternity and sorority kids, that's what they looked like — started just smashing their heads. The kids were sitting down, in front of a hotel, in front of Gene McCarthy's headquarters. I remember seeing this young man in a suit and tie carrying a young woman in a nice dress and she had blood pouring out of her head. And this total stark look of disbelief on his face.   *Jane*

Somebody said the famous words, "The whole world is watching" — and it became a chant.   *Tom*

The whole world saw that on TV, but to have seen it up close and personal, it was one of the things that made you feel that the war really was coming home. It really was in our own back yards now.   *Alice*

It really was a police riot, it truly was a police riot. Daley, and whoever was giving orders, were clearly out of control.   *Jane*

Before the convention we had done a lot of work with some of the McCarthy people, trying to get them to join us in some things and support demonstrations we were planning and they didn't really want to have anything to do with us. And five days later, we were sort of in the trenches together.   *Carol*

By the end of the night delegates from the convention, hundreds of them, came back and joined us — and they were carrying candles.
So by the end of the week the liberals from the inside and the anarchists on the street and the cultural revolutionaries and the anti-war people — everybody seemed unified in this incredible revolt against what happened.
                   Tom

There are moments when it seems like the raw outlines of certain parts of the society are just laid out to see, and they're visible in ways that they are just not visible other times. And Chicago was one of those times, when the potential of our society to tip over to a police state, when the nature of a police state is just laid out in front of you. There it was, up close and personal.   *Jane*

NIXON

In November, Richard Nixon edged out Humphrey by a fraction of a percentage.

The Democratic Convention in 1968 was really in some ways a watershed. Hubert Humphrey was nominated on a pro-war, prosecute the war platform and then Nixon was elected.

Nixon was going to end the war by winning it, he was going to end the war by intensifying it — it became clear that that's what he was about. At that point is really seemed like there was no legitimate way to end the war. It was intensifying, it was escalating ever more. So all routes to legitimate challenge seemed to be closed off, against what seemed to us to be the popular will, at least as the media represented it. So there was this enormous frustration.   *Jane*

This was a time when the country really seemed to be imploding. There was a sense that none of the normal means could work — petitions, peaceful demonstrations — that we were really heading into a situation where we really didn't have much recourse but to defend ourselves, literally.   *Alice*

We were headed suddenly into the years of Nixon — and the war was going to get worse. At home, the situation was going to get worse. Nothing that we could do was going to reach those idiots who were running our government. The war was just going to keep on and on and on.   *Carl O*

CHICAGO 8

The repression against the anti-war movement increased, in the courts as well as the streets. In Chicago, eight activists were indicted on conspiracy charges related to the demonstrations.

Nixon thought that by putting us on trial, and a lot of other people on trial around the country, that it would have a chilling effect on young people and restore law and order. Just the opposite actually happened.

There's a secret memo from J. Edgar Hoover, the director of the FBI in late 1968. "A successful prosecution of this type would be a unique achievement at the Bureau and should seriously disrupt and curtail the activities of the New Left." So there was this intent to go back to the [Joseph] McCarthy period, thinking that if we were arrested, tried, and convicted it would curtail the activities of the New Left. It had no such effect, it was more like putting fuel on the fire.

It made us convinced that we were obviously being put on trial as symbols, so we have to act as symbols. We don't want to be symbols of cowardice or intimidation, so we'll be symbols of defiance against this, which will thwart their real goal which is not just to put us in jail but they want to demoralize everybody and curtail the activities. *Tom*

Bobby Seale is gagged and bound to his chair and dragged from a court of law. What does it say about our society and what does one do in response?

Bernardine

Black Panther Bobby Seale was removed from the case and the eight defendants became seven. After a long trial, most were convicted, only to have the convictions overturned on appeal but not before they spent time in jail.

When I got to Santa Barbara in 1969, I was surprised at the degree to which many students were attentive to that trial. The student government invited Bill Kunstler, lawyer for the Chicago 8, to speak at UC Santa Barbara. It was after his speech that a large group of students were coming out of the stadium where he'd spoken — probably the biggest political event ever to occur up to that point at Santa Barbara — that police attacked the crowd and sparked this reciprocal fighting back that ended in a trash dumpster being pushed into the local Bank of America branch building in the community, which set fire to the building. And since the police by this time had withdrawn and the firemen delayed coming in there, the bank burned down and that became a world-wide news event.

Dick

When you look back at what happened in 1968, it hardly justifies our tremendous arrogance and cruelties and divisiveness — but it does set a context and a framework for the extremes, for the desperate way in which we tried to figure out what was right and what we should be doing.

Bernardine

12
COINTELPRO

We later learned we were targets of the FBI's Counter-Intelligence Program, or COINTELPRO as it was called.

Like the students at Columbia going through the files at the president's office, it took some people in a tiny town in Media, Pennsylvania, to break into the FBI office [in 1971] and start sending the files to *The New York Times* to discover that the FBI and the Justice Department and the US government had a massive program called Counter-Intelligence Program — COINTELPRO.

Bernardine

And it's true, although we didn't know it at the time, that the FBI was beginning its infiltration of the left, of the anti-war movement at that time, with a program called COINTELPRO.

Carl O

After Watergate, Senator Frank Church and others started to investigate the role of the FBI in repression during the '60s — and the role of the CIA as well.

Dick

There was a whole operation that was organized within the Department of Justice, called COINTELPRO, Counter-Intelligence Program, which was devised specifically to destroy the peace movement and the civil rights movement. It was the same strategy under which they smeared Dr. King and attempted to plant people in all different organizations who would carry out really provocative entrapment activities.

Sue

94TH CONGRESS }
2d Session }   SENATE   { REPORT
                                                          { No. 94-755

INTELLIGENCE ACTIVITIES AND THE
RIGHTS OF AMERICANS

BOOK II

FINAL REPORT

OF THE

SELECT COMMITTEE
TO STUDY GOVERNMENTAL OPERATIONS

WITH RESPECT TO

INTELLIGENCE ACTIVITIES
UNITED STATES SENATE

TOGETHER WITH

ADDITIONAL, SUPPLEMENTAL, AND SEPARATE
VIEWS

APRIL 26 (legislative day, APRIL 14), 1976

Church Committee Report, 1976

In January 1975, the Senate resolved to establish a Committee to:

conduct an investigation and study of governmental operations with respect to intelligence activities and the extent, if
any, to which illegal, improper, or unethical activities were
engaged in by any agency of the Federal Government.[1]

This Committee was organized shortly thereafter and has conducted
a year-long investigation into the intelligence activities of the United
States Government, the first substantial inquiry into the intelligence
community since World War II.

The inquiry arose out of allegations of substantial wrongdoing by
intelligence agencies on behalf of the administrations which they
served. A deeper concern underlying the investigation was whether this
Government's intelligence activities were governed and controlled
consistently with the fundamental principles of American constitu-
tional government—that power must be checked and balanced and
that the preservation of liberty requires the restraint of laws, and
not simply the good intentions of men.

The FBI had an index of people who were considered national security
risks, to be rounded up in case of a national emergency and incarcerated
without trial. COINTELPRO went further than that, it literally targeted
people for "special action" and many if not all of those listed as national
leaders of SDS, I think we eventually learned, were on the COINTELPRO
lists.   *Dick*

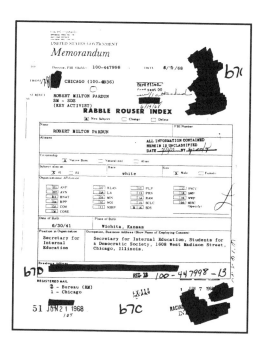

At the time we all thought, myself included, that there were a lot of agents and informants around but since we thought we had nothing to hide and we were an open movement, it really didn't matter very much.   *Tom*

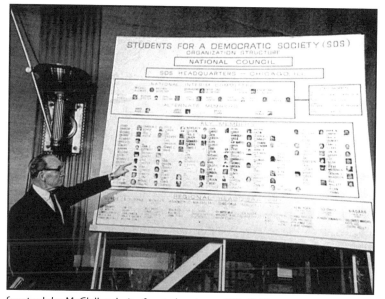

Senator John McClellan during Senate hearing on SDS, 1969

One of the things we were really unprepared for was the extent of FBI and law enforcement retaliation against movement activities at the time. We knew there would be police infiltrators and infiltrators from the FBI, we knew that there would be surveillance. We had no idea of the depth of it.

Mark

---

fbi investigates sds

FBI investigators have been uncovered inquiring about SDS activities at Yale and Wesleyan in the past week. At Wesleyan, they approached the Dean for a membership list, and were turned down. At Yale they asked SDS member's roomates for information about their activities, beliefs, and character.

Wesleyan SDS reports that their public statement on the inquiry has reinforced the chapter, and has shown up the FBI. The Dean's public attack on the FBI has helped that. 8 members of the chapter in a letter to the editor of the Wesleyan **Argus** stated that they had nothing to hide, suspected the investigation to be an outgrowth of their recent fast for peace in Vietnam, and exposed the FBI attempt to get their "information" by devious means.

The New York **Times** broke the story on Tuesday the 19th.

The FBI investigation, as reported in **New Left Notes** two weeks ago, seems to be nationwide and based on a general "checking-up" motivation rather than a specific political intention, at least for the time being.

New Left Notes, April 1966

We had a special relationship with our Austin Police 'Red Squad', particularly Lt. Gerding who was assigned to follow us everywhere and take pictures of us. From the time we began, Bert Gerding was kind of a fixture. He'd come to meetings and sit there taking notes in the back. It was very out front.

Alice

We thought at the time that we'd be able to somehow tell who the police spies were in our ranks, and we learned — very bitterly — that it wasn't nearly so simple. In Los Angeles, we learned after a lawsuit against the Police Department for spying on progressive organizations that a police spy had not just become friends with but had become the lover of a movement organizer and moved in with her and spent 18 months living with her. She never knew what happened until this came out in the course of the lawsuit. I cannot imagine a deeper feeling of betrayal and a deeper feeling of invasion than something like that.

Mark

SDS calls itself a radical organization. Radical means going to the roots, going to the values. But the system comes down against us because our values are a threat or a challenge or a different set of values than the values on which these institutions are structured.

Cathy Wilkerson, interview, 1968

Our paranoia was no match for what they were really doing. In our wildest imaginations, we thought: they're too sophisticated to actually sit down in a meeting, at the highest levels, and figure out how to destroy us; this is all just happening at a local level, and so on and so forth. We really didn't realize, we absolutely did not realize, how extensive and coordinated and directed the program was to try and undermine us.   *Mike*

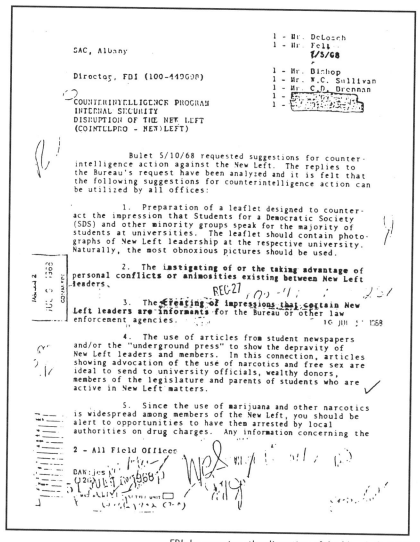

FBI document on the disruption of the New Left, 1968

fact that individuals have marijuana or are engaging in a
narcotics party should be immediately furnished to local
authorities and they should be encouraged to take action.

6. The drawing up of anonymous letters regarding
individuals active in the New Left. These letters should
set out their activities and should be sent to their parents,
neighbors and the parents' employers. This could have the
effect of forcing the parents to take action.

7. Anonymous letters or leaflets describing
faculty members and graduate assistants in the various
institutions of higher learning who are active in New Left matters.
The activities and associations of the individual should be
set out. Anonymous mailings should be made to university
officials, members of the state legislature, Board of
Regents, and to the press. Such letters could be signed
"A Concerned Alumni" or "A Concerned Taxpayer."

8. Whenever New Left groups engage in disruptive
activities on college campuses, cooperative press contacts
should be encouraged to emphasize that the disruptive
elements constitute a minority of the students and do not
represent the conviction of the majority. The press should
demand an immediate student referendum on the issue in
question. Inasmuch as the overwhelming majority of students
is not active in New Left matters, it is felt that this
technique, used in carefully selected cases, could put an
end to lengthy demonstrations and could cause embarrassment
to New Left elements.

9. There is a definite hostility among SDS and
other New Left groups toward the Socialist Workers Party
(SWP), the Young Socialist Alliance (YSA), and the
Progressive Labor Party (PLP). This hostility should be
exploited wherever possible.

10. The field was previously advised that New Left
groups are attempting to open coffeehouses near military
bases in order to influence members of the Armed Forces.
Wherever these coffeehouses are, friendly news media should
be alerted to them and their purpose. In addition, various
drugs, such as marijuana, will probably be utilized by
individuals running the coffeehouses or frequenting them.
Local law enforcement authorities should be promptly advised
whenever you receive an indication that this is being done.

11. Consider the use of cartoons, photographs, and
anonymous letters which will have the effect of ridiculing
the New Left. Ridicule is one of the most potent weapons
which we can use against it.

12. Be alert for opportunities to confuse and
disrupt New Left activities by misinformation. For example,
when events are planned, notification that the event has
been cancelled or postponed could be sent to various
individuals.

You are reminded that no counterintelligence
action is to be taken without Bureau approval. Insure that
this Program is assigned to an Agent with an excellent
knowledge of both New Left groups and individuals. It must
be approached with imagination and enthusiasm if it is to be
successful.

As an economy measure the caption "COINTELPRO - NEW LEFT"
should be used on all communications concerning this Program.

We didn't know at the time, of course, about COINTELPRO, and we didn't really know that there was an FBI strategy to disrupt — by harassment, arrests, constant disruptions, constant disinformation, constant creating of divisions, and constant court appearances and trials and meetings with lawyers. But we felt it, we experienced it.   *Bernardine*

INTIMIDATION AND HARASSMENT

In the course of the Church investigation an investigator came to see me in Santa Barbara and said, "I've been authorized to show you documents from the FBI about you in the COINTELPRO program." And what she showed me was a telegram asking that I be targeted and particularly proposing that an anonymous letter be sent to the trustees at the University of Chicago detailing my involvement with SDS and related activities. And it was signed "concerned alumus" — however they misspelled alumnus. Not only was that proposed, but authorized personally in the hand of J. Edgar Hoover and he said, "Perhaps this can get Flacks removed from his position."   *Dick*

The level of surveillance and law enforcement pressure on the National Office got a lot more severe. We received an anonymous phone call from a tipster who stated that he was calling us from inside the US Department of Justice and that the SDS National Office was going to be raided. That night we got a phone call saying, "The fire department is on its way." And before we could even say, "Who is this?" they said, "Get out of the building, the building's on fire." And they hung up. There was banging on the door. We looked out and there were hook and ladder trucks lined up all around the block and they were putting the three-story ladders up against the building and firemen and FBI agents or some kind of men in suits with grappling hooks were pulling the hinges off the front door of the building.

They said, "We have to come in, we received a report that the building's on fire." We said, "The building's not on fire, there's no fire here." And they said, "We have to come in and see for ourselves." Well, you had about 60-70 heavily armed men out there — armed not only with firearms but with hooks and hatchets. We said, "We'll let in a delegation, two of you can come in." They charged in, arrested 5-6 people. Of course there was no fire, not a puff of smoke anywhere. The guys spent the night in jail, charged with resisting arrest, interfering with a fireman — and eventually most of the charges were dismissed.   *Sue*

Dave Slavin, Tim McCarthy, and Mike Klonsky getting out of jail.

Urgent **RAIDS** Urgent

Pigface Mitchell and the Justice Department gang are planning to begin a nationwide series of raids and arrests of as many as 500 people at over 50 cities and campuses within the next 10 days. The Man is moving to spread terror and to isolate the movement from the people, using the lie that "disorders" are the work of a handful of militants rather than the consequences of decaying imperialism and the inability of the state to meet the jad needs of the people.

SDS has been informed by sources within the administration that Attorney General Mitchell has the backing of Congress to institute a series of arrests directed at local leadership on phony charges ranging from sedition to narcotics. The average sentences they are shooting for will range around two years, with the minimum goal of six months—the immediate objective being the removal of these activists from schools and cities through the summer and especially through the fall. These arrests will be carried out by local law enforcement agencies; the charges will be city and

The National Office of SDS was raided early Monday morning, May 12, by Chicago pigs and firemen who broke through the front door and brutally attacked staff people and SDS members. Five brothers were dragged off to jail as they tried to protect the National Office from destruction.

Arrested were Michael Klonsky, National Secretary; Tim McCarthy, NO staff; Ed Jennings, UICC Chapter; Les Coleman; and Dave Slavin, New York regional staff. They were charged with absurd charges, ranging from "battery on an officer" to "interfering with a fireman" and "inciting mob action." Bail was set

When this raid on the SDS office happened, I had an infant daughter who was there in the office with us. When we saw that they were getting ready to break the doors down, we really thought they might kill us. We didn't have any weapons — we had a couple baseball bats and they were intended for when people broke in to steal purses, not for combat. I took the baby and hid her in a carton behind the sink in the darkroom. And we pushed some kind of a desk up against the darkroom door to make it look like that was the end of the office because we really thought they might come in and start breaking heads.   *Sue*

> An arrest of these people is part of the systematic attempt to divert attention in this country from the war and from racism, and to focus it on some mythical enemy inside this country — the student movement, young people who are protesting the war and racism
>
> *Bernardine Dohrn, press conference, 1968*

We had an office in the Silver Lake area [of Los Angeles]. The building is gone now — at one point it was fire-bombed. I remember getting a phone call that the building was burning down and driving there frantically, not knowing if people were inside or not, and not being able to get inside the perimeter, surrounded by fire hoses and fire trucks. Nobody was hurt — everybody got out — but the building was gutted.   *Judy*

The repression was widespread, it was personal, it was close. We didn't call it COINTELPRO because we didn't know that's what it was called. We knew about the Red Squad. We knew they broke into our apartments and we knew they took one of our leading members and hung him out the window by his legs and threatened to drop him if he didn't cease some of the activities he was involved in. We knew they jailed one of our people and took away his asthma medicine and left him for two nights in a jail cell to die. So these were not things that were far away for us, these were things that were very close to us.   *Bill*

When national demonstrations were held in Washington, DC, we would help coordinate them. During that time, the program to undermine us, COINTELPRO, was in full bloom. In our regional SDS office the phones went dead for three days before every national demonstration that was held in Washington that year. And the phone company, when we would call, would just say, "Oh, we just seem to be having troubles on the line." It was quite routine.   *Mike*

DIRTY TRICKS

For all the overblown sense of ourselves, we underestimated the government strategy against us. We saw it quite clearly against the Black Panther Party and against the black liberation movement, but underestimated the level of disruption that was going on directed at us.   *Bernardine*

> The purpose of this program is to expose, disrupt, and otherwise
> neutralize the activities of this group and persons connected with it.
>
> *FBI Counterintelligence Program memorandum, May 9, 1968*

The following memorandum from Robert Pardun's FBI file gives
some details on the COINTELPRO program.

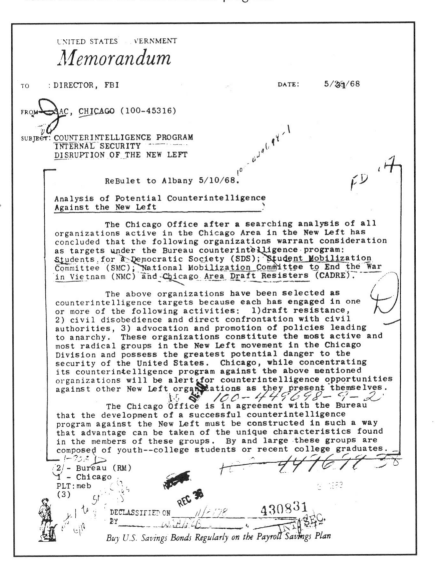

UNITED STATES   GOVERNMENT

Memorandum

TO   : DIRECTOR, FBI   DATE: 5/31/68

FROM : SAC, CHICAGO (100-45316)

SUBJECT: COUNTERINTELLIGENCE PROGRAM
INTERNAL SECURITY
DISRUPTION OF THE NEW LEFT

ReBulet to Albany 5/10/68.

Analysis of Potential Counterintelligence
Against the New Left

      The Chicago Office after a searching analysis of all
organizations active in the Chicago Area in the New Left has
concluded that the following organizations warrant consideration
as targets under the Bureau counterintelligence program:
Students for a Democratic Society (SDS); Student Mobilization
Committee (SMC); National Mobilization Committee to End the War
in Vietnam (NMC) and Chicago Area Draft Resisters (CADRE).

      The above organizations have been selected as
counterintelligence targets because each has engaged in one
or more of the following activities: 1)draft resistance,
2) civil disobedience and direct confrontation with civil
authorities, 3) advocation and promotion of policies leading
to anarchy. These organizations constitute the most active and
most radical groups in the New Left movement in the Chicago
Division and possess the greatest potential danger to the
security of the United States. Chicago, while concentrating
its counterintelligence program against the above mentioned
organizations will be alert for counterintelligence opportunities
against other New Left organizations as they present themselves.

      The Chicago Office is in agreement with the Bureau
that the development of a successful counterintelligence
program against the New Left must be constructed in such a way
that advantage can be taken of the unique characteristics found
in the members of these groups. By and large these groups are
composed of youth--college students or recent college graduates.

2/- Bureau (RM)
1 - Chicago
PLT:meb
(3)

REC 36

DECLASSIFIED ON _____   430831
BY _____

Buy U.S. Savings Bonds Regularly on the Payroll Savings Plan

They have in general discarded any pretense of observing the
codes of morality previously accepted by youth in the U.S.
It is felt, therefore, that it would be useless to attempt to
discredit or embarrass these groups by publicizing their sexual
immorality.

Similarly, members of the New Left organizations do
not regard an arrest record as a discredit if the arrest occurs
in connection with civil rights, anti-war or draft resistance
activity. On the contrary, the person arrested is held in
higher esteem by his peers and is viewed as one with a "real
committment." Disinterest in law and order and an attitude toward
law enforcement officers bordering on contempt appear to be traits
common to all individuals active in the New Left. These individuals
when arrested for crimes growing out of civil disobedience, draft
resistance and related activities appear to thrive on the television and newspaper coverage afforded them. Therefore, it is
felt that a counterintelligence program should be very select
in the individuals it attempts to neutralize or discredit through
exposure, and only those individuals should be selected for
exposure who are guilty of the type of activity that would discredit them with the New Left movement or would discredit the
New Left movement in the eyes of the public.

The Chicago Office feels that the tremendous success
of the Bureau's counterintelligence program against the Communist
Party, USA (CPUSA) was possible because of the Bureau's extensive
informant coverage of the CPUSA for many years at every level.
Through the Bureau's high level informant coverage a vast amount
of knowledge was collected concerning the thinking and activities
of all the leaders of the CPUSA. This knowledge made it possible
for the Bureau's counterintelligence program to pinpoint and
exploit the weaknesses of the CPUSA.

Also, :   Chicago feels that it is very fortunate in having
promising extensive coverage of the New Left and key activists
activity in the Chicago area, and feels that through utilizing
the knowledge being developed through this program it will be
able to develop an aggressive and imaginative counterintelligence program. In order to utilize this informant coverage to
the fullest possible extent, the Chicago Office is at present
carefully examining all of its New Left informant files to
determine if one or more of these informants could be used on
a full-time basic.

As the Bureau is aware, most New Left leaders,
particularly those active at a national level, devote full
time to their responsibilities and Chicago feels that it must
have informants engaged full-time if it is to achieve the
success in the counterintelligence program it desires. Through
full-time informants the Chicago Office will be able to
learn of and be in a position to exploit the subtle differences
and clashes of personalities that could disrupt and hamper the
New Left movement.

Appropriate recommendations regarding any informant found
possessing the requirements suitable for his utlization in
the New Left movement on a full-time basis will be submitted
under the individual case captions of the informants.

Recommendations

Experienced agents of the Chicago Office who have
conducted investigations in the New Left movement since its
inception recommend the following counterintelligence Program:

1. That the Chicago Office continue in every possible
way to see that quick and decisive prosecutive action is taken
against all members of the New Left for all violations of law.
It is believed that prosecutive action is most effective in accom-
plishing the desired disruption of the organized activity of these
groups.

Chicago will continue to follow closely the activities
of all individuals engaged in the New Left movement to uncover any
possible violations of law committed by these individuals.
Particular attention will be given to possible violations of the
Selective Service Act and any violations of local law concerning
which the police may take action.

With respect to the above, the Bureau is requested to note that during the latter part of 1966 ████████ (BUfile 100-439955,CGfile 100-39357) was convicted for violation of the Selective Service Act and subsequently was released on ████ appeal bond. The Chicago Office in closely following this case, especially ████████ day-to-day activities, recently determined that ████ had been arrested both in California and New York while participating in anti-draft activities. This information was immediately furnished to AUSA DAVE HARTIGAN, USA's Office, Chicago, who in turn filed a motion with U.S. District Court Judge JAMES B. PARSONS, Chicago, to revoke ████ appeal bond based upon the fact that ████ had left the jurisdiction of the court without permission.

b7c

In view of the above, Judge PARSONS revoked ████ appeal bond and ████ was ordered into immediate custody on May 27, 1968, to begin serving a four year prison term.

2) That the Chicago Office institute action to disrupt the SDS national convention scheduled to be held at Michigan State University, East Lansing, Michigan, June 10-15, 1968, by attempting to insure that one or two leaders of the SDS are unable to attend the convention. The individuals who would undoubtedly play leading and significant roles at this convention and in any programs adopted at the convention are:

b7c

ROBERT MILTON PARDUN, Internal Education Secretary of SDS

The absence of one or more of the aforementioned individuals is certain to create confusion at the SDS national convention.

The Chicago Office is currently conducting an intensive review of pertinent laws and statutes of the State of Illinois, Cook County and the City of Chicago to ascertain if the SDS National Office or the aforementioned individuals may be in violation of any regulation which could permit the issuance of a subpoena to one or more of these individuals requiring that they appear at a hearing within the State of Illinois during the period of the SDS national convention June 10-15, 1968.

The Bureau will immediately be advised of the nature of any law which could be utilized for the above described purpose.

In addition, as the Bureau is aware, the Chicago Office continues to enjoy excellent relations with the Chicago Police Department. ████████

b7c
b7D

One of the broad provisions of City Ordinance 193-1 proscribes "Any unreasonable or offensive act, utterance, gesture or display which under the circumstances creates a clear and present danger of a breach of peace or imminent threat of violence."

The blacked-out name in paragraphs 1 and 2 is Jeff Segal.

3) That the Chicago Office be authorized to contact Internal Revenue Service (IRS) on a local level regarding the income tax returns of key activists in the Chicago Division to determine if they have submitted federal income tax returns and if so have made any fraudulent entries as compared with known background.

The following key activists are located in the Chicago Division:

b7C

b7C

BUfile 100-447549
BUfile 105-157629
BUfile 100-443916

BUfile 100-440138
ROBERT MILTON PARDUN, BUfile 100-447998
BUfile 100-447957

It is noted that all of these individuals have been active in the leadership of New Left organizations and that they have been involved in the financial transactions of these groups. It is not believed that their financial records will bear close scrutiny and the possibility exists that they may not have filed any tax returns in recent years.

The IRS is already conducting a searching examination of the financial records of SDS and it is believed that IRS would be happy to extend its examination to include the income tax returns of the above mentioned key activists.

If the IRS could uncover violations of the law in the tax returns of these key activists any legal action brought against them would disrupt the New Left movement because these individuals are the driving force in the organizations with which they are affiliated.

The Chicago Office can assure the security of this IRS contact if approved.

4) That the Chicago Office turn over to IRS financial information it has obtained concerning

Investigation has revealed that   and
who identified themselves as

b7C
b7D

It is recommended that information concerning the   be turned over to IRS because it is believed   represents taxable income   and which should have been reported on their 1967 federal income tax return. If IRS determines that   and   did not file returns for 1967 or that they did not include this money as income, the Chicago Office feels that IRS will be in a position to take action against them under the federal income tax laws.

b7C

Chicago will give aggressive and continuous attention to this program and remain alert for any situation or development offering the potential for counterintelligence action.

The FBI had some successes and some failures. Jeff Segal, SDS's national draft coordinator, was grabbed from what he was told would be a short 'routine' hearing on May 27, 1968, and sent to jail for more than two years. On the other hand, Robert Pardun and the two other national officers presumably referred to in the FBI document on page 184 all arrived safely at the SDS convention.

The Internal Revenue Service response to a request for information on Robert Pardun follows.

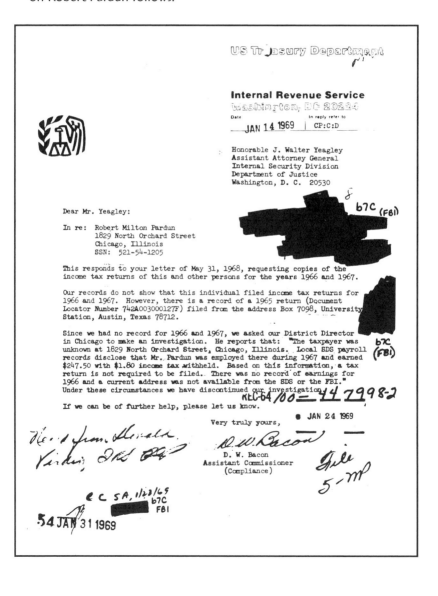

I think there was a lot of police activity — fomenting divisions, fomenting rumors, promoting weird and divisive relationships.   *Sue*

They'd call people and say, "Did you know so-and-so was sleeping with so-and-so?" in order to get people angry and mistrustful. "Did you know that so-and-so said something about you that was bad." That was one of the key things they did — to try and create disunity and distrust amongst us by spreading those kinds of rumors and tales.   *Mike*

In this period in NY & Columbia, we would have meetings and there was this fellow who would come called 'Crazy George,' who wore this Greek Trojan headdress and would always say, "Well, you guys are chicken and aren't ready to do real action. Everybody who wants to plant bombs, everybody who wants to do real stuff, I'm going to pass around a piece of paper for everybody who wants to have a meeting of the really tough people." Crazy George would pass this sign up list around and people would sign with their address and phone numbers and he'd have his private little meetings. It turned out later that he was a government agent. He was setting up the youngest and most naive kids.   *Jeff*

I saw suspicious provocations in Chicago and heard about others. I knew enough history to know police agents liked to infiltrate militant organizations — and to act more militant than thou, in order to bring down the righteous wrath of public opinion as well as police power against the militant movement. So I wrote an article, right after the Democratic convention, for the *San Francisco Express Times*, under the headline "Casting the First Stone," which I began by saying: watch out for the first person to throw a stone, he might be a cop.   *Todd*

I was in the National Office when we received a set of cartoons that were aimed at Bernardine Dohrn. Bernardine was pictured in the cartoon as lying on a beach in Cuba surrounded by bags of money, or something along that line, the idea being that she was personally profiting from her role as a leader and therefore people shouldn't trust her.   *Mike*

There was a cartoon that came out about me. At the time we thought it was from an opposing sectarian group, which was what we were supposed to think — that is what 'dirty tricks' are all about and why dirty tricks are so effective.   *Bernardine*

WOMEN: EQUAL OPPORTUNITY TARGET

I had a series of experiences, particularly in the women's movement, of people who I trusted and loved who turned out to be some kind of agents. There were splits that I know were exacerbated. And then I got my FBI and CIA records — blacked out everywhere. And you knew when you read those records that these are people you knew and trusted and that these splits just didn't happen by accident. There were really wedges put in there. It had happened at *Off Our Backs*, it had happened in Washington women's liberation, it had happened in the women's movement. And we later learned about COINTELPRO.

Marilyn

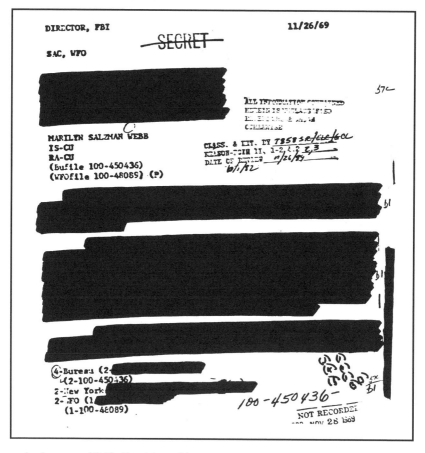

In January 1969, President Nixon was inaugurated. And there was also a 'counter-inaugural' organized by the Mobilization Against the War to protest Nixon's inauguration.

I just want to set the stage of what this counter-inaugural was like. There was a huge circus tent. It was freezing and it was raining and there was mud everywhere — and there were 20,000 people in this tent. The Mobilization Against the War was convinced they had to have some women on this podium.

I was 26 at the time — we were very, very young. I had been a movement organizer at that time for 4 years. This was my first speech at a major event.

I got up to talk — and you have no idea how mild this speech is. When I look at it now I think: this is so pathetic. It was like, "We have to take back control of our bodies, we have to be able to get jobs, we have to be able . . ." Whatever it was, it was so mild. And fights, fist-fights, broke out down there and people were screaming down there and they were yelling at me on the stage, saying, "Fuck her!" "Take her off the stage!" "Fuck her down a dark alley." And then people were hitting each other for saying that. And that was my debut.

I got home and the women from my consciousness-raising group were at my house and also a lot of women who had been staying there because they had come to Washington from other places. My apartment was packed with people and we were sitting there, trying to figure out what had just happened and what we were going to do, how we felt about the fact that these were our brothers, essentially, and why did this happen. What had we done wrong? Did we not give our speeches right? What had we done? What was wrong here?

And the phone rang and this person at the end of the phone said, "If you or anyone like you ever gives a speech like that again anywhere in the country, we'll beat the shit out of you." I thought it was Cathy Wilkerson. It was her voice. And I was appalled.

We never saw each other again until an SDS reunion in 1988 and I was so shocked to see her. I had no idea how her life had gone or what was happening with her. And by that time Todd [Gitlin] had written his book, *The Sixties*, and he had put down this story in the book and at the time I said it was Cathy. And Cathy came up and she said, "You know, Marilyn, it wasn't me. I didn't call you."   *Marilyn*

I was dumbfounded because, as far as I was concerned, I never made a phone call like that. In fact, I didn't know about Marilyn's speech until later and I remember hearing something about it and being horrified at what had happened.   *Cathy*

I felt a chill go through me because, on the one hand, I didn't know whether to believe her and, on the other hand, I had enough experiences at that point in the movement to know that it may have been true, that it wasn't her. And I'm still feeling this chill right now as I'm telling this story.

Marilyn

I was surprised when Marilyn and I finally spoke about it because I was not one of the people at that period of time who was promoting or glorifying violence. That was not my personal thing. I was a militant, there was no doubt about it. And I would throw over a ROTC table at the drop of a hat — and I would squirt shaving cream at men in tuxedos. But I was not about personal violence in that sense in any way. So it was astonishing to me that Marilyn would believe that. But in retrospect, I can understand why, given the chaos of the time, given everybody's defensiveness and how threatening the differences in political positions were.

Cathy

My consciousness-raising group had been meeting for one and a half or two years. Cathy Wilkerson was in the group and had been my friend. Cathy was very against a separate women's movement and was very, very critical of my moving more and more towards just doing women's activities — and I saw this as my constituency.

Marilyn

I recognized that there had been tension in the women's group in Washington between women going in the direction of radical feminism and women in SDS. When we talked about it, Marilyn explained that those tensions within the women's group provided for her the context within which she was willing to believe that the phone call was from me. I could understand in that situation, when everything was so loaded, that she could make that jump.

For the COINTELPRO people, or whoever made that phone call, it was a very strategically and well thought-out phone call.

Cathy

The impact of it was to split the women's movement into a separate movement because we decided at that moment that we really did need to separate. We needed to have our own identity and that we would not find support until we were strong enough that it would come. And that we needed to have our own agenda and yes, we had international concerns but we had to deal with them ourselves, as a women's movement, and with other women internationally, but not in the left the way it had been structured.

It was a very, very important phone call that really was the division that ended up with a separate women's movement.   *Marilyn*

ATTACKS

Sometime after the Sixties were over, I made a request through the Freedom of Information Act, for documents that the FBI had kept on me. And, at the rate of ten cents a page, I couldn't afford to get all of the records they had kept on me — not because I was of such significance to them as an individual person but because I was one of the national officers of SDS.

Amongst those documents was one which was truly frightening. The director of the FBI, J. Edgar Hoover, had sent a memorandum to the Chicago office directing them to follow me 24 hours a day — to keep track of where I was every minute of every day. The fellow in Chicago who was supposed to carry out this order, wrote back saying: J. Edgar, I don't think you quite realize, but this fellow doesn't sleep at the same place every night, he's constantly on busses, traveling to campuses, he's going here, he's going there, he's doing all these things and it's very difficult to follow him 24 hours a day. And back came a memorandum that said: I meant what I said. Not only do I want him followed 24 hours a day, but your job is to neutralize his effectiveness in the movement. What was frightening about that was that the term 'neutralize' really meant everything from doing physical harm to me, to beating me up, to trying to stop me from being able to speak, all the way up to the possibility of killing me.   *Mike*

May 5th, 1969, was the day I was assaulted.   *Dick*

Dick was in his office at the University of Chicago and someone came in from behind and smashed his skull in with a hammer and used the claw of the hammer to try to tear his hand off. And he was just left there. We got a call from Mickey [Flacks] and met her at the hospital and really didn't know if Dick would live.   *Vivian*

I spent a month in the hospital and a long recovery time after that.

We had assumed right from the beginning that this had something to do with my political role. The police, for some reason, insisted that it had no connection to known hate groups that were operating in Chicago at the time.

Years later, a reporter for *The New York Times* found out that I had been targeted by COINTELPRO and he called me and said, "Are you the same Dick Flacks who was at the University of Chicago and who was beaten at the university?" I said , 'Yes." And he said, "Well, what's the connection between that and the fact that you were an FBI target?" I said, "I don't know." I don't think I had thought of it in quite that way.

That article in *The New York Times* prompted me to pursue getting my FBI files under the Freedom of Information Act. The first response was very minimal, lots of stuff missing and lots of stuff deleted. We pursued the files for a long time and under court order I was delivered a very large carton of files. What wasn't there was any paper that linked the FBI to the attack on me.

The FBI had all this information about me but the most important thing that ever happened to me, the way I became most public in the world — this attack on me at my office at the University of Chicago — nothing but a newspaper clipping in their file. They had no other information about it.

Well, the judge had ordered them to supply me with an index of every document and we were able to see from that that there were documents from the time that I was assaulted that they hadn't supplied and we asked the judge to supply some of those. The judge then released to me a particular document which said that an informant — a 'previously reliable informant' — had told the FBI, after my assault, that members of the Chicago Police were involved. And the report concludes, "We no longer consider this a reliable informant."   *Dick*

The truth is we don't have the whole story. I got, through the Freedom of Information Act, 22,000 pages of files going back to the late '50s when I apparently wrote some editorial questioning J. Edgar Hoover. And the agent went to the neighbors of my parents in Royal Oak, Michigan, and they reported that as far as they knew I was a totally loyal 19-year old American. So it started early. Most of the 22,000 pages were blacked out. So all of the damning and shocking things that I found have to be laid against what might have been in the black-out, which was three-quarters of the documents.   *Tom*

I haven't seen my unexpurgated files but I think that before a bottom line can be drawn on the experience of the Vietnam period, the FBI's going to have to come clean.   *Carl O*

13
Unraveling | *1968–1969*

In the midst of all this, SDS began to unravel.

The war did not seem to be stopping. I think a lot of us did not realize how effectively we had broken the back of the American military impetus and how it was going to be forced to wind down. We were ignorant of that, all we saw were the endless killings and the endless bombings.   *Mark*

What the violently non-violent confrontational mobilizations accomplished, as it turned out, was to convince a great number of the war planners that if they went on with the war, at least if they went on with the war the way they'd been doing it, they were going to wreck the country. They were going to derail their power eventually. So, in that sense these confrontational tactics were effective.

However, at the same time, they were also heading the movement towards a kind of recklessness and self-enclosure in which many people who were opposed to the war were also horrified by the direction of the movement — horrified by the tactics and also horrified by the very cavalier and rather ignorant, spectacularly naive views that were beginning to develop about the wonders of third-world revolution. And what both the tactics and the often naive and often disingenuous views about communism eventually did was to seal off the movement.

So that paradoxically, as the movement was becoming effective, I would argue, in limiting the magnitude of the war and making an ending politically possible, at the same time, the movement itself was walling itself off from America. So that in a certain sense the anti-war movement is both a heroic and tragic sacrifice. It accomplishes a great deal against the war — but it also slits its own throat, it also collapses what had been a promising left.

So one has the paradox, according to public opinion polls, that as the war becomes more unpopular, so does the anti-war movement.   *Todd*

The TV coverage of the war was overwhelming, it was just overwhelming — and we were mesmerized by it.

By 1968, every night on TV we were watching children running through the streets of Vietnam with napalm on their bodies, burning up. Every night on TV we watched a day's worth of body bags being loaded on to the planes, being shipped home.   *Cathy*

The war kept going, and kept going, and kept increasing, and kept killing more and more people, and kept becoming more and more senseless, and more and more outrageous. The feeling of urgency was really palpable — the whole country was being annihilated and we couldn't do anything about it. So there was that enormous, enormous, frustration and rage and feeling of helplessness.   *Jane*

The war was so horrendous, it was so heavy, it was so immoral. The things we did to those Vietnamese people were just beyond comprehension. We destroyed over 50% of the villages of South Vietnam; half the population was refugees; 600,000 women were prostitutes, 50% of the mangrove swamps had been defoliated; 50% of the forests were destroyed — by bombs, defoliants, or whatever. There's land mines; there's the use of pellet bombs against the people.

It's horrendous what we did to them, all in the name of anti-communism and democracy. What else could we have done — we the anti-war movement — but oppose it with everything we had.   *Robert*

WHAT DOES IT TAKE TO STOP THIS?

Peaceful protest wasn't getting us anywhere. I think it was a really painful debate, and also very frightening, because it raised the stakes so high. And I remember getting to a certain point and feeling so desperately that something needed to change, that the war couldn't go on, that things couldn't go on like this, that I felt that my life was worth risking in order to make this stop.   *Elizabeth*

You cannot have an open heart and watch television and see young men from your country killing and strafing civilians, mostly unarmed; you can't watch footage of people dropping bombs over civilian populations, who've posed no threat to the United States at all, on a daily basis; you can't see photographs of people being napalmed — and not think, "My God, what does it take to stop this?"   And when you couple that with the people who are coming back here in tatters, not just physically but emotionally wrecked by what this had done to them, it was just clear in every way that this had to be ended.   *Mark*

As the fighting went on and the variety of air munitions changed, including napalm bombs and anti-personnel exploding fragment bombs, we felt that we were in the situation of German civilians during World War II, that our government was committing atrocities in our name and we desperately felt the need to not be 'good Germans.'   *Bob*

We'd grown up with *Life* magazine picture of concentration camps — and that seared everybody.   *Jane*

We asked ourselves: if you had been a German during the Second World War, what kind would you have been? A 'good' one — an obedient to the fatherland German — or would you have raised some hell, and tried to gum up the war machine by any means necessary. If you could have stopped the Holocaust? Of, course, nobody questions that, I would have done anything. And so, people with the best of intentions, I believe with absolutely pure intentions, came to the conclusion that they had to take actions that they would have found unimaginable a few years earlier, because they would do anything to, as they describe it: bring the war home, force the United States to address this war, right here.   *Sue*

Some in SDS began to talk seriously about new ways to respond to the continuing war.

For us the stakes seemed to be getting very high — and we felt called upon to up the ante. So going into 1969 there were tremendous debates about how to up the ante, about what that meant.   *Cathy*

The idea was to force the issue, in the United States — to make people look at the fact that young people, students, were developing a tremendous amount of anger and rage about what our country was doing and which side our country was on.   *Elizabeth*

There was an enormous amount of anger that what was now majority opposition to the war seemed to have no effect on government officials — and the sacrifice of Southeast Asian lives and American lives continued. And so we were onto the notion that we had to escalate and that we had to make the cost of the war at home great enough so that the people in Southeast Asia and American troops who were forced to go to fight in Vietnam were not paying the only cost.   *Bernardine*

It seemed like every single person in Vietnam was going to be massacred by the time this was over. We felt that if we could take some of the heat from what was going on over there and re-direct the enormous rage of the American government towards some of its own in this country that it would make a difference in what happened there.

The idea was that if we could start a second front in this country, then we would divert some of the resources of the FBI, the CIA, the Army, the Department of Defense from their efforts in Vietnam or their attacks on the black community.   *Cathy*

We felt at that moment in time that it was essential to put your body on the line; that people around the world were dying at the hands of our government — our military and our police forces — and if you rested on your privilege as white people, as students, as youth, you were collaborating, you were participating.   *Bernardine*

Young men who resisted the draft and young men who went into the army in both cases were taking enormous risks and making enormous sacrifices, and obviously the civil rights people in the South had taken risks and made enormous sacrifices. So we felt we also had to take risks. For us, how that played out was raising the level of militancy.   *Cathy*

I thought the more militant demonstrations, the concept of 'bringing the war home,' might stop the war — that if we could make the country ungovernable, we might stop the war. In fact, J. Edgar Hoover sent a memorandum to the president saying that if he continued to send more people to fight in Vietnam, he [Hoover] could not guarantee the safety of the country. In other words, the war at home could get so big that it became ungovernable. And that, I think, was a possibility.   *Robert*

The more they said, "We know we have the support of the vast majority of the American people," the louder we wanted to say, "No you don't!"

Cathy

AROUND THE WORLD

In the middle of all this, lo and behold, the radical spirit is globalized. There is the movement in France which brings the government to a standstill. It has a romantic, utopian, surreal quality, which is alluring, enormously thrilling to us. It seems like they're about the same thing we are.

The Mexican students are on the march — and slaughtered.

The Czech students resisting the Russians also felt sympatico to us. 'Welcome to Czechago' was a slogan at the time.   *Todd*

We were part of a global upheaval around revolution, liberation, justice and equality.   *Bernardine*

The world was aflame — and we had to find out what our role in it was.

Carl D

In August 1968, I led a delegation of thirty people to meet with the Vietnamese in Eastern Europe. It's hard to remember this but there were very few Vietnamese nationals in the United States during the '60s. Vietnamese were not allowed to come to the United States, so we had no access to meeting with the Vietnamese except outside the country.

We went first to a conference in Lubliana, Yugoslavia, of students from all of Europe, the New Left — students who had just come from the French rebellion, from German SDS*, students who were underground in Franco Spain at the time, and some who had been through a year of opposing Tito's attempt to control the universities in Yugoslavia. We had an incredible week of meetings there, overshadowed by the Soviet invasion of Czechoslovakia.

We then went to Hungary and spent ten days meeting with a delegation of thirty Vietnamese in Budapest. For me, the experience of meeting Vietnamese citizens — teachers, soldiers, organizers, bureaucrats — was utterly transforming. Having worked for a year as a full-time organizer, I

---

*Although not connected to the US organization, the German SDS, *Sozialistischer Deutscher Studentenbund*, resembled SDS in many ways.

don't know how I didn't know, but until I got to know Madame Van, who was the woman I spent the most time talking with, a young women my age, I didn't think through what occupation of a country would mean — how everyone had lost family members, how everyone traveled to get there by living days in tunnels, by walking hundreds of miles to get to an airport where they could fly to Eastern Europe.   *Bernardine*

Tom Hayden, Vivian Leburg Rothstein, and Rennie Davis examine anti-personnel weapons in Vietnam, 1967.

The conference in Bratislava [in 1967] deepened my understanding of the war and of the human side of the war — and also of the importance of the anti-war movement. I really saw how we fit in internationally and that what we were doing in terms of the anti-war effort was not only significant within the country but it was also significant outside the country.

I'd been very against the war and involved in lots of anti-war activities but here I was talking to Vietnamese, talking to them about their experience and sharing with them our experience and it was pretty amazing. And the Vietnamese were just so wonderful that I think we were all very moved by their compassion, by their wisdom, by their grace.   *Carol*

What Madame Van and the delegation of Vietnamese told us about was their daily life. They told us about living under relentless B-52 bombing and the strafing of the countryside, the napalming of the forests and of the cultivated rice fields of Vietnam, the threatening of the dike system, the history of the national integrity of Vietnam and how long it had been threatened by Chinese and other invaders — and how the United States was just one piece. By telling us their history, they also told us the detail of their lives: the people among them who lived full time in tunnels in an underground world to escape the bombing, the people who had lost their entire family to the American military, people who had seen their friends and relatives transformed into beggars and prostitutes around US military camps, the vulgarization of Vietnamese culture in the image of the Americans — women curling their hair and putting silicone in their breasts to appeal to American GIs.   *Bernardine*

They had a sense of strategy: the American military strategy will fail, the political strategy in South Vietnam will fail, we will make the Americans leave. It was so thorough-going in a very strong sense of: your job is with your government. Your job as Americans is to not let the government do this in your name.

And they would say to us, "Tell me about your mother, what does she think?" They didn't want to know about how many students I'd organized at Columbia University; they wanted to know what middle America thought and how we thought we were going to move the majority of the American people.   *Bernardine*

ESCALATION OF RHETORIC

All the pressures changed the tone of the debate.

We were caught up in the escalation of rhetoric, tactics, militance.

Bernardine

There was a process of one-upmanship on rhetoric that was not healthy. Eventually it one-upped us right out of touch with either students or the mass of the people.   *Bob*

There was an escalation of rhetoric, and of revolutionary commitment, on the part of individuals who hadn't been heading in that direction until quite recently. Part of it was just the pressure of the whole group trying to move history forward, trying to really make something happen. If you really want to end the war, if you really want to change American society, we have to try harder, we have to raise the ante, we're not trying hard enough. And there's an element of truth in that. It was not a time for half-way lame measures. You needed a lot of commitment, there was a certain amount of personal risk. And so people kind of cheered each other on, nudged each other on, cajoled each other into making a bigger commitment.   *Sue*

The language of the movement is significant in charting certain kinds of growth and mistakes and changes that took place. The language of the early days was a language of community and inclusion and love and beloved community, and that language was solid and good and important. But it also needed some depth to it.

The more we knew, the more we learned, the more we understood. We began to situate American racism, for example, not just in a history of slavery, which was important, but in a history of capitalism — and in an understanding that the system we were talking about was a capitalist system and an imperialist system. The more we situated the Vietnam War not as a mistake of American policy but endemic to American policy, the absolute logical conclusion of a great empire on the rise, a neocolonial empire on the rise, the more we turned to sources like Marx to understand certain aspects of it.   *Bill*

It seemed to us in that period of time, that we were in a different situation. We were no longer talking about resistance and we were no longer talking about opposition to a war, but that these issues were all connected and that the opportunity was here not just to support revolutions in other parts of the world but to really transform American society.   *Bernardine*

Robert Pardun with flag at SDS convention, 1968

There was a lot of talk about revolution during that period of time and some people thought we were right on the doorstep of revolution, that if we just pushed a little bit harder that the people would rise up against the government and that we would have a fundamental re-shuffling of the situation in this country.

I talked about revolution, I'm not going to say this was other people, I talked about revolution. But inside, I knew that it was not a revolutionary situation. I always came to the conclusion that we had a lot more work to do, that we were not in a revolutionary situation.   *Robert*

We were wrong. It wasn't a revolutionary situation, but it looked like a revolutionary situation and it seemed analytically like there was a lot of evidence. We convinced ourselves because there was a lot of evidence for the thesis that this was a revolutionary situation.   *Bernardine*

Part of the madness, the extremes that occurred, was because while it was a progressive movement, it was not in touch with average everyday Americans. It doesn't matter what you think, if you want to change society, it matters what most people think. So if it's going to take you a longer amount of time to change other people's minds, you have to accept that.

Juan

We felt small and insignificant in the face of these enormous war crimes that were happening and we needed guarantees of success. So different groups of young people latched on to different periods of history. There were people who thought that what happened in Algeria — and we all watched *The Battle of Algiers*, which was a very significant movie to us— was the critical piece. Some thought that what happened in the Russian Revolution in 1917 was the critical piece; others the Chinese Revolution. Others of us read Regis DeBray and what happened in Latin America with Che Guevara and the *foco* groups. There were a wealth of revolutionary examples. And, of course, always there were the Vietnamese fighting for the right to self-determination.   *Cathy*

As these cadre organizations developed within SDS, those folks saw our role as being a leadership vanguard of the movement. And if you're going to be a leadership group, you have to know where you're going and you have to have a strategy for getting there. So it's critically important that you have a correct analysis and a correct strategy.   *Jane*

PROGRESSIVE LABOR

At the same time, Progressive Labor had moved into SDS as a disciplined Leninist cadre, with the aim of basically taking it over.   *Jane*

There are always left-wing groups around who on their own cannot grow big. What they do is they come into what they think of as a mass organization and try to push it in a direction that they approve of. This happened with SDS. A relatively small group, the Progressive Labor Party, saw SDS as a mass arena within which to recruit and a mass movement that they hoped to influence. They were Maoists, that is followers of Mao Zedong thought.

Bob

Progressive Labor was an organization that grew out of a split inside the US Communist Party around 1960. They launched a youth arm which they called the May 2nd Movement. They were originally a very vibrant, dynamic group. At a certain point what they hoped the May 2nd Movement would become was what SDS was actually becoming. So they saw it as their revolutionary duty — or tactics — to dissolve May 2nd Movement and to join SDS as a group.

Carl D

We felt like we needed easy solutions and we needed clear answers and we needed simple answers for a situation that was not simple.

Cathy

They had a plan, they had a strategy they could lay out: this is what we need to do. So if you were sort of against the war and becoming increasingly frustrated, anybody with a strong strategy had some appeal.

Sue

One of the reasons PL was effective was that they were serious, they weren't 'wimpy,' and at least in their rhetoric and in their vision, they weren't short-term. They were drawing serious students from serious places because they were serious. And we felt a need to be as serious. And so what became cartoon-like in terms of various Marxists throwing slogans at each other had a kind of serious basis — and the serious basis was struggling for what direction the organization ought to take.

Bill

I had been originally somewhat sympathetic to them. I felt, originally, that PL raised a needed voice that spoke in favor of approaching the traditional working class, a pro-labor point-of-view and that it wouldn't hurt SDS to have this strong working-class perspective brought into it. I related that to my own background and that's why I was somewhat sympathetic to them. But at a certain point PL went through its own internal change and made a drastic shift in course. Originally they had been great supporters of the national liberation movement and had supported people like Che

Guevara and Malcom X. Now they had decided to come out and take a radically ultra-left turn that also at the same time completely took an anti-nationalism point-of-view. So they went off in a weird sectarian direction.

Carl D

The beef that we had with the Progressive Labor Party, or at least one of them, was: this was the time when the Vietnamese had forced the United States to sit down at the bargaining table in Paris to negotiate a peace agreement. And naturally when you're negotiating, there's got to be some give and take, and some compromise. And there's a war going on and thousands of people a day in Vietnam being slaughtered. Progressive Labor Party denounced the Vietnamese for negotiating with the United States, characterized them as selling out to United States imperialism. We thought: who are they, they're not fighting this war, so who are they to tell the Vietnamese how to fight this war and bring it to a conclusion that they can live with? They want to fight to the last drop of Vietnamese blood, but they're not the ones over there.

Sue

Although Progressive Labor was never a large proportion of SDS, and was mostly active in certain key chapters, they had a disproportionately large influence both in those chapters and in national meetings.

One consequence of their internal organization is that once their line had been set amongst themselves, all their people inside SDS were compelled to carry it through and to try to organize SDS to go in their direction. *Carl D*

It wasn't their ideas — SDS was open to ideas — it was the methods that they used, the way they controlled meetings. Every Progressive Labor person who stood up said the same thing as the last Progressive Labor person who stood up. So you would hear this one viewpoint over and over. It was like a tape recorder when they would talk — and they all had the same tape. And you couldn't talk them out of anything, you couldn't reason with them. And that just made people very angry because it would tie up whole meetings.

Robert

They were disciplined, they were organized, they had a set of slogans and a set of resolutions they were bound to support — and everybody else is out there voting their conscience, voting with their little group of friends, not well-organized.   *Sue*

One thing that PL people had was a rather elaborate coherent ideological vision and our folks would be arguing against them in campus chapters or national meetings with a 'soft' language of democracy.   *Bob*

Our old form of wide-open committee of the whole ways of organizing and of doing business could not withstand that kind of organized group working inside us — people who had a line, who were going to push it, who would use every tactic in the book, of which there are many, very well developed, very well-honed, to push it through. And we were defenseless in our old organizational form to fight that.   *Jane*

As my friend Merle Hansen out in Nebraska used to say about organizing farmers, "Organizing farmers is like trying to organize a wheelbarrow full of frogs." Well it's the same way with SDS chapters — they were a wheelbarrow full of frogs in lots of ways. And if you went in with a small core of people who were disciplined and had a plan, then in the midst of a wheelbarrow full of frogs you could do some interesting things.   *Carl D*

The leadership of SDS that was not part of those sect groups then felt that it had to have something to compete with, that it had to have the more militant language, it had to have the more daring program, it had to have the more confrontational stance than the self-styled Maoists did. And so, largely out of reaction, I think, to the presence of these infiltrating forces, and largely in an effort to cut out a separate turf to rally people to, the non-sectarian leadership became more and more extreme in its own thinking.

Steve

We had to differentiate ourselves from Progressive Labor within our own organization. They claimed to be revolutionary Marxists, so we said: wait a minute, you guys aren't revolutionary Marxists, we're the revolutionary Marxists. But to prove it we had to go cite chapter and verse — and that's where the rhetoric came from.   *Carl D*

When SDS went into Weatherman and PL factions, both extremes were wrong. Both neglected the fact that what made SDS strong was its mass appeal. Both became dogmatic, both became sectarian, and both became totally divorced from reality.   *Juan*

After I left the National Office in 1968, I went back to the University of Texas and the SDS meetings that I went to were totally different than the SDS meetings that I'd been at in Austin a year previously. There was a Progressive Labor group in the Austin chapter and it just made the meetings dysfunctional.

Robert

Wherever there was a PL chapter, once PL took over a chapter, usually pretty much everyone else left it, sooner or later.

Carl D

YOU DON'T NEED A WEATHERMAN . . .

The Weathermen came from the best of SDS — and it was horrifying to me to watch people that I had been so close with decide that the continued escalation of the war required an escalation by the movement. If the war effort was going to get bigger and more violent, then the movement had to get more violent. This is how the Weathermen came to be.

Carl O

The group of people who eventually became the Weathermen were among the smartest, nicest, most attractive human beings in the organization and at first I thought: this is great, this is going to be a formation that will resist the sectarianism of the Progressive Labor Party. But gradually they got stuck, in my opinion, in the negative spiral of increasing the radical rhetoric.

Bob

They didn't go crazy. They are the same people that I was in the beginning of the '60s. They were just the inversion because of what we had all gone through in such a short period of time.

Tom

Although very few in SDS actually became Weathermen, the frustration and rage that they felt, and that led to their formation, were shared by many. And their actions greatly affected all of SDS.

What brought us together was an absolute determination to hurl everything we could at the ability of the American government to make war.

In that spring [1969], a group of us began to meet to talk about how we wanted to define ourselves politically within the organization and that led to what came to be known as the Weatherman document.

The document was called, "You Don't Need a Weatherman to Know Which Way the Wind Blows." It's a line from Bob Dylan and it was meant partly as a joke and partly why would you write fifty impossible-to-read pages filled with the densest kind of rhetoric and then name it something whimsical like that. But in any case, that's the way we all were.

The document was an attempt to put our politics into the debate with Progressive Labor and with other factions within SDS. What we argued essentially was that we had to define and see the struggle going on in our country as a world struggle, and that it wasn't simply a group of intelligent intellectual students who were involved in this but it was actually a struggle that had dimensions that reached far beyond the borders of this country. We defined it as a struggle of the third world against America, against imperialism, which was being led by the American government, the American military and the American ruling class.

And so we saw ourselves situating ourselves as allies with that third world rebellion. We saw America as a big octopus with its hands all around the world, eight big claws all around the world, and third world liberation movements like Vietnam, like Cuba, cutting off tentacle after tentacle — and that our job inside the mother country was to ally with those forces as powerfully as we could.   *Bill*

14
Demise of SDS | *1969*

Spring and early summer of 1969, SDS was really quite dramatically cracked into several fragments. And those divisions were fundamental — around the question of the war and around the question of white and black in America.

Bernardine

The break-up of SDS is, in some ways, harder to analyze than the fall of Rome. At least in the fall of Rome you can talk about drinking water out of lead pipes and the lead getting into their brains and making them a little wishy-washy on certain things. SDS was somewhat more complicated than the fall of Rome.

Several things were happening here simultaneously. One was the building up of frustration over not being able to make any major breakthrough in ending the war. A second thing was the infiltration of some organized Marxist-Leninist sects — at least they thought they were Marxist-Leninist sects, I don't think that's what they were at all. And the third thing was probably help from the government. But all of those things conspired to set an intense factionalism going in SDS.   *Steve*

Six months ago we were all one happy family of radicals. We had differences, but now we were at each other's throats.   *Carl D*

So SDS was sent into a turmoil. An organization that was fundamentally democratic and very inclusive became in 1969 a warring ground of all of these different viewpoints.   *Cathy*

We succumbed to that kind of divisive splitting and certainty that we were right.   *Bernardine*

Bernardine Dohrn, 1968

1969 SDS CONVENTION — CHICAGO

All the divisiveness came to a head at the SDS national convention in June, 1969.

We went into the convention prepared to fight it out ideologically.

Bernardine

When we got to the Chicago Coliseum on the first day of the convention, we found that somebody — the FBI or the [Chicago Police] Red Squad — had sharp-shooters and photographers arrayed on the rooftops of the buildings across the street, watching the entrance. We were not unaware of the fact that there appeared to be guns trained on us. It was a pretty intimidating atmosphere.

Sue

PL came in numbers far greater than their proportion in SDS. Others coalesced into a bloc calling itself the Revolutionary Youth Movement (RYM), which included the Weathermen. And many, many others were not aligned with either of these — some attending their first SDS convention.

We were well aware that a split was in the making, or that sharp differences were going to surface. What I expected was an attempt by Progressive Labor to take over the organization.

Sue

Bernardine Dohrn at SDS convention, 1969

The convention was contentious from the start and ended with an organization bitterly and irrevocably split.

The RYM group and their followers, led by Bernardine Dohrn, walked out and reconvened, declared themselves the real SDS, elected officers, and 'expelled' PL.

That led to an absolute split, a walk-out, insane debate. The operation was a success and the patient died. We thought that SDS was going to continue after that but the splits were fatal.   *Bernardine*

It was true madness that gripped us. It was a theater of the absurd. I sat in the balcony and watched it and cried as these things happened.

There was a huge movement going on and we're down in there, this few hundred of us, doing this huge psychodrama, thinking that it was important.   *Jane*

And a lot of people were saying: can we get out of here and go get a beer someplace? It's too confusing, too much bullshit. So I think what you had was that a lot of people who weren't in any of the various factions or blocks that were starting to develop got turned off to this. This is not what they came here for — and they couldn't analyze it, they couldn't process it.   *Sue*

There was mass confusion at the periphery. What's going on? Who are these people? You say to some 19-year old that SDS is now a revolutionary organization and the 19-year old from Muskegan, Michigan, says, "What?"   *Bob*

And then you also had infiltrators and people who were there just to provoke.   *Sue*

After the convention, the RYM group returned to the SDS office in Chicago. The PL/SDS group opened an office in Boston but never succeeded in attracting a large following.

CUT LOOSE

The vast majority of SDS people listened to the debate and just said: I think I'll just go home and do what I do best, which is to work locally.   *Robert*

There were people who detached themselves emotionally, who went home saying, "Well, that's over. I'll find another way to fight." They were not so much heart-broken, as some of the founders of SDS were, as really befuddled by it, confused by it. And they decided to stick with local organizations from there on out — and not try to relate to a national organization. I'm not sure very many people left that convention knowing what the split was really about.   *Sue*

Soon after the convention, the Revolutionary Youth Movement split again — into RYM I/ Weatherman and RYM II.

What I did not foresee, and I think many of us didn't foresee, was that there was going to be a whole other split — and that was between us and the faction that came to be known as the Weathermen.   *Sue*

Once Weatherman evolved, SDS pretty much ceased to function as a mass organization.   *Juan*

People then went off. The Weather people went off to do what they did and various disciplined cadres emerged, each trying to create the correct line. And a lot of us just were cut loose. That was the end of SDS in my mind.   *Jane*

People who had been our best, most valued friends took different paths than we did — and we didn't talk to each other for more than a decade after this split occurred. That was painful.

For us, the issue was: if you resort to certain kinds of actions you'll get isolated from the American people, from the majority of the students, who are willing to go pretty darn far but there are certain things that cross a line that most people can't cross. So it was personally painful and I think politically inevitable, the product of both the external political conditions we were dealing with and this immaturity, this inability to sort things out into gradations and an inability to compromise, to be flexible tactically, inability to unite with people with whom you had serious differences. I don't say that because I think we were wrong in rejecting a strategy of violence and terrorism, I think we had to reject that. But I don't think we knew how to argue the right way about this. And in the heat of the moment, things happened very fast.   *Sue*

I'm deeply sorry that political differences led to personal cruelties. I ended up being personally mean with old friends with whom we had disagreements. Nobody felt able to escape the criticisms. There's a lifetime of regrets for that. Harm was done.   *Bernardine*

In the summer of 1969 when a whole bunch of us were arrested and sentenced to thirty days in jail for another Columbia protest, six of us ended up in a county jail in New York at the very time that SDS had its historic convention when it broke into the Progressive Labor faction and the Revolutionary Youth Movement faction, and then split off into the Weathermen. So the six of us were in jail, and every faction was represented in jail. While they were having their convention, we were having our battle in jail over the same issues.

I decided that when I got out, I was leaving SDS — and I was going to go back to East Harlem, back to the Puerto Rican community to try to build something with our own community that would provide some sort of a progressive direction, taking some of the important lessons I'd learned in SDS but leaving behind all the baggage.   *Juan*

These folks that I had been so close to, suddenly I felt cut off from — and I didn't know what was happening any more in this movement that I had loved for so many years of such intense action.   *Carl O*

I dropped out and fell away from the whole dynamic. People like myself huddled up, trying to keep each other warm while this movement we had believed in tore itself apart and went berserk. It took me a long time to try to work out the dynamics of what happened there and to try to understand individuals, people I'd been close to and who I'd thought of as sensible and warm people, who were speaking in tongues, who were spouting absolute nonsense.   *Todd*

It was an extremely dispiriting time for a great many of us. I know I was facing serious burn-out during that period — and I didn't know what to do.
Carl O

TWO, THREE, MANY MOVEMENTS

While SDS was disintegrating, other movements were growing. Freedom is contagious.

The women's movement, by this time, was going full steam but women were not the only ones to be energized and inspired to create new movements in the late 1960s — or to feel conflicts with the 'mixed Left'.

The Farmworkers' Union had been organizing Latinos in the fields of California for a number of years. Various Latino groups, including the Young Lords, began in other places. In August 1970 a number of groups sponsored the National Chicano Moratorium against the war.

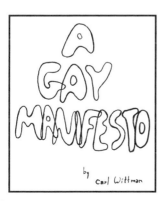

A month after the 1969 SDS convention, the Stonewall Rebellion in New York kicked off the modern gay liberation movement. At the end of that year, Carl Wittman, a long-time SDS activist, wrote A Gay Manifesto.

> In the past year there has been an awakening of gay liberation ideas and energy. How it began, we don't know; maybe we were inspired by black people and their freedom movement; we learned how to stop pretending from the hip revolution. Amerika in all its ugliness has surfaced with the war and our national leaders. And we are revulsed by the quality of our ghetto life.
>
> Where once there was frustration, alienation, and cynicism, there are new characteristics among us. We are full of love for each other and are showing it; we are full of anger at what has been done to us. And as we recall all the self-censorship and repression for so many years, a reservoir of tears pours out of our eyes. And we are euphoric, high, with the initial flourish of a movement.
>
> *Carl Wittman, A Gay Manifesto*

The American Indian Movement (AIM) was founded in 1968.

In April 1970, the first Earth Day was held, heralding — or confirming — the start of the environmental movement.

In a move that would become very important in ending the war, Vietnam veterans were also organizing — not only for an end to the war but also around issues that particularly affected them such as better medical care for wounded vets, compensation for damage due to Agent Orange, and help for post-traumatic stress. Vietnam Veterans Against the War (VVAW) was formed in June 1967 and grew steadily. Soldiers still in the army rebelled as well, in a variety of ways. Alternative GI newspapers were starting up on bases around the country

15
Weatherman

NOTE: This chapter continues to explore the actions and thinking of a relatively small group of people within SDS who eventually became the Weather Underground. I am including so much about them here because of their impact on SDS — and on the public perception of that era.

As some chapters and members pulled away, the Weathermen, elected to the leadership of SDS at the 1969 convention, increased their militancy.

The Weather grouping was a numerically small group of people. They were exceptionally skilled leaders with great regard in the organization, but very small in numbers. When they took over the National Office, they had already, however, given up on the idea of a mass student movement as a progressive force.

Bob

VIOLENCE

I always respected nonviolence. I never thought it was a bad strategy but I always had reservations about whether it was enough. It didn't seem like it worked for the Native Americans.

Cathy

One of the barriers that went down for me was the barrier crossing into using violence. This was not a dominant idea in SDS at all, but I don't think SDS was ever a pacifist organization, I don't think it ever took up the issue and I don't think the issue ever presented itself as viable and real until the end of the decade. Then the violence on leaders of the black movement; the violence of Vietnam, which was so regularly visited on society; the violence of politics at the top of our national life, with the president being killed and the candidate for president being killed and people being shot — and violence was introducing itself pretty powerfully.   *Bill*

We came at the question of violence in a very uprooted way — and it was a real dilemma. Nonviolent attempts had failed. We had this enormously successful nonviolent movement in this country and still we felt that it hadn't done the trick, it had been a drop in the bucket. Now, in retrospect, we see that is far from the case, that the bucket was overflowing. But at the time it felt like it had not been enough.   *Cathy*

I was drawn to pacifism but I was never an ideological pacifist. I came to feel very strongly that violence existed in certain relationships — and while that violence was not usually expressed, it was a quiet unacknowledged violence. But when you had relationships of slave and slave-master or dominant invading country and cowering people who are having their land and their lives stolen, that is violence! And if the people resist, or if the slave stands up, then we hear a chorus of people saying, "Oh, there's violence, that's violence." But in reality the violence was in the relationship.

What we see today, again and again, is violent deaths quietly executed. We see kids dying of preventable disease, we see people on the streets, we see people who can't have meaningful work. This is violence. And once that was part of my consciousness, and once the war escalated out of control, it seemed to me only reasonable to not just support the Vietnamese willingness and ability to shoot down American B-52s that were dropping bombs on them — it seemed reasonable for us to stop the B-52s from taking off. After all, they were right there in California. We could walk up to the fence and throw rocks at them, so why couldn't we climb over that fence and put a small charge in the engine. And so we did. That felt like, though it was crossing a barrier, it didn't feel like a barrier that was so huge that it was insurmountable.   *Bill*

The issue of violence is complex. And how could we not be complicit? How could we, by virtue of who we were and the color of our skin and the country within which we were born, not be complicit with the violence that was already going on? There were no nonviolent options the way that we saw it.   *Cathy*

We wanted to confront people on a daily basis with the same kinds of issues that people were being confronted with in Vietnam.   *Elizabeth*

When one says the movement turned violent, I look back at it and think it turned militant, and the language was certainly violent. The reality was really largely symbolic violence. It was largely mass demonstrations that involved throwing rocks and pushing and shoving with the police; it involved beatings by the police; and it involved events that were militant but popularly understood and welcomed as theater, almost pranks — the destruction of empty ROTC buildings on campuses.   *Bernardine*

GETTING READY

Summer of 1969 we knew we were moving more intensely towards confrontation and towards a crisis with the government, with the war. And we knew that we were ill-prepared to do that.   *Bill*

We organized ourselves into collectives in the spring of 1969.   *Bernardine*

Our emphasis was on remolding ourselves as human beings to become self-sacrificing, risk-taking in the way that the Vietnamese were. We were profoundly affected by that.   *Cathy*

We used it to try to change ourselves, to be ready for a struggle that we felt was going to get more and more serious, to make ourselves ready to be better fit for the struggle, to shed the ways in which we came to the struggle filled with the values of the larger society.   *Bernardine*

In Detroit there was a park where the Hell's Angels were having a picnic and we marched in with our Viet Cong flag flying — and the Hell's Angels weren't having any of it so they beat the shit out of us. But afterwards we had some good talks with some of them because they thought we were pretty cool to be willing to come in and be that confrontational. It did take a certain amount of courage, as well as a certain near-sightedness. Simultaneously we were having ongoing conversations about what was required of us in this period, what do we personally have to do, and we were building a sense of disciplined collective living towards the revolution.   *Bill*

DAYS OF RAGE — OCTOBER 1969

I had been told there'd be 5000 people; there were more like 500.

Elizabeth

But we went ahead anyway. We had announced that it was a national demonstration — and we were going to have a national demonstration no matter who showed up.   *Bill*

Then the leadership led us running out into the streets. That in and of itself wasn't so surprising because we had been doing a lot of demonstrations in the streets. But this was different: it was small, it was night, everybody was wearing helmets. It had this very foreboding — and to me completely confusing — aura to it. But I was down with it because I didn't know what else to do, and I wanted to do something, and I wanted to be confrontational because I couldn't live with myself and the knowledge of what was going on in the world if I wasn't.

We were running through the streets. We were targets for the police who immediately, of course, came. Somebody started breaking windows, with sticks they broke car windows and store windows on the first couple of blocks. We were surrounded by police. Everybody ran in every direction. Some people got arrested, some of us got away.   *Cathy*

For me the thing that really ended it was that they were smashing Volkswagens. Had they been smashing Cadillacs, I would have gone along with it. But Volkswagens seemed to be the car that anyone who didn't have much money would drive. I thought: well, that's really misdirecting the anger.   *Elizabeth*

By that point in '69, SDS had shed large quantities of its membership because of its chaotic, confrontational stance. On the one hand, there was campus organizing going on which I was involved in. And on the other hand, in the Days of Rage in Chicago the message was: if you're not out with us in the street, you're an awful person, you have no moral integrity, and you have no right to exist on the face of the earth. Now this is not a good organizing stance. And it was very self-righteous, judgmental, arrogant, elitist, etc..   *Cathy*

We weren't really reaching students with the popular message anymore, we were turned inward arguing with ourselves and each other.   *Bernardine*

Was it successful? No, absolutely not. People got arrested, people got hurt. What I think is unfortunate is that as people look back on that period they see things like Days of Rage as characteristic of the student movement when I think it was more unusual. There was an aspect of Days of Rage that was violence for violence sake — and to the extent that people see the student movement and the movement against the war as that rather than all the wonderful things it was, it's too bad.   *Elizabeth*

FRED HAMPTON ASSASSINATED

The next step for us was the murder of Fred Hampton and Mark Clark.
Bernardine

Fred Hampton was the leaders of the Chicago Black Panther Party, a very young, charismatic community leader with a real community focus.   *Cathy*

Fred Hampton had been the president of the NAACP youth group in Maywood and was very helpful in creating dialogue with young white kids about race. For a number of the kids I worked with, he was the first black person they'd ever met.   *Vivian*

We knew Fred Hampton and Mark Clark well. The Black Panther Party office was three-quarters of a mile down Madison Avenue from the SDS office.   *Bernardine*

Fred Hampton was killed December 4, 1969. He was the godfather of my daughter, Jennifer. We were very good friends.   *Sue*

I remember sleeping in somebody's apartment in Chicago on the couch and being woken up at five o'clock in the morning and being told that Fred Hampton had been killed and a little about how he had been killed although the details were not clear at that point. And it was definitely one of those moments.   *Cathy*

We had moved back to Los Angeles in the fall of that year. We got a phone call early in the morning informing us that Fred Hampton and Mark Clark, another leader of the Illinois Black Panther Party, had been shot to death while asleep in their beds in their apartment.   *Sue*

He was murdered by the Chicago Police Department in the most brutal, vicious, assassination.   *Vivian*

The police had an informant drug him ahead of time, they stormed into his apartment, they riddled his bed with bullets.   *Cathy*

Hundreds and hundreds of bullets in the door of his bedroom, while he was lying in bed, and all around his bedroom, so that his body was lying in a pool of blood.   *Vivian*

They were murdered. They weren't just attacked, just set up, just indicted — these were things that were happening to lots of people. They were murdered in cold blood.   *Bernardine*

And simultaneously that night and that weekend on the West Coast and in the Midwest there were other raids on the homes and offices of members of the Black Panther Party in which a number of other people were killed and injured.   *Sue*

That was powerful for us, that told us what was in store for us if we were serious, if we wanted to stand in Fred's shoes, if we wanted to stand with the Vietnamese against the bombs that were manufactured here, that were built here, and the planes flew from here to drop them off. Then we had to figure out what does it mean to stand next to those folks.   *Bill*

There was a wake for Fred Hampton and I took my students, who loved him. And there he was in this church in Bellwood, dressed as a Black Panther with his black jacket and black beret and the Panther Party newspaper under his arm and his beads and his rifle — and I almost passed out right in his casket. For one, to see him dead, this incredibly dynamic, very young — he was in his early twenties — young man assassinated in our own town.

It was a way in which leadership, particularly black leadership, was just nipped off before someone could really develop a constituency. I knew about Malcom X and I knew about Martin Luther King — but this was someone I actually knew. It was very close to home.   *Vivian*

I think our sense of our own powerlessness was really brought home very vividly. We spent a lot of time asking ourselves: what could we have done, what should we have done, what's an appropriate response, how could we respond to something this terrible.   *Bernardine*

You felt you could not protect the people that you loved and it felt terrible, it felt really terrible. And, of course, you could be next — but in a way it was worse to live with the responsibility that you couldn't protect people. It just added to this profound sense of responsibility that I think we were feeling about the course of history and the course of our country's history. And I think it led many people to desperate political tactics because they could not absorb and accept and live with their own powerlessness.   *Vivian*

Panthers were getting killed and shot at right and left. And we, as white students and organizers who believed the same things that they did, were not getting killed and shot at. So we felt that we had to put ourselves in a position where we were taking the same risks and putting ourselves in the same jeopardy as young men who had to go into the army and were fighting in Vietnam, as young men who chose to resist the draft, as people who were in the Black Panthers, people who were in the South still fighting. It wasn't right that we could be protesting and not be taking the same risks as they were. It was not honest and it did not have integrity to it.   *Cathy*

It sent people into all kinds of political contortions that made no sense, it sent some people into military adventurism because they were tortured by all this going on and they couldn't do anything about it.   *Vivian*

I think it was so difficult for us to take the step of saying that we were not going to accept the violence of the United States government in Vietnam or against the Panthers — by any means necessary. From our training and our history as a democratic popular organization, that step was very unbalancing for everybody.   *Cathy*

I had a fairly strong and fatalistic sense that I would be killed in the movement and that the more steps we took towards serious opposition, the clearer I was that I would be killed. It felt personal, it felt immediate, up close — but there was a kind of determination to walk into it.   *Bill*

By 1970, and by the time Fred had been killed, and the assault on the Panthers and COINTELPRO had really become widespread and affected every city, the roof blew off the concept of militance.   *Cathy*

Bill Ayers, Ann Arbor, 1968

CLOSED

The Weathermen tightened their ranks and lost interest in the bulk of the membership that was still on the campuses.

There was a lot of assessment that went on, but it went on under the pressure of the gun, it went on with a lot of our people being arrested, multiply, some of our people being beaten pretty severely by the Chicago Police, our apartments being raided and people being dragged off to jail, friends and comrades being held out windows by the Red Squad, and really tortured in some ways, as intimidation tactics, not even to get anything. We were being infiltrated massively by the FBI and the Chicago Police. So it was an intense couple of months. But within that there was a lot of thinking and re-assessing.

I remember one part of the conversation was people losing faith that the student movement could go much further, that we could transform ourselves much more into a serious force that would contend for power. I remember other people feeling much more strongly that there was still a lot of reliance that we ought to give to the mass movement and to the upheaval of students on campus. And I remember an argument that the tactics of the government and the police were getting more repressive, more deadly, more serious, and that if we were going to survive, even as an oppositional force, we should prepare the capacity to survive arrest, murder, assassination and all that.   *Bill*

We decided that part of what we had to do was go underground. Part of what had to be done was to build a clandestine apparatus. We decided it based on some understanding of what other struggles in the world were doing and did under these kinds of conditions — and partly based on an unwillingness to spend the next three years on trial.   *Bernardine*

I remember two arguments there. One was: we will all be slaughtered because we are serious and they are serious. And if we're not as serious as they are about surviving, we will certainly all be killed. That was one argument. A second argument was: look at where the movement's going — the Chicago Seven Trial, the this trial, the that trial. Do we want to spend the next ten years organizing self-defense things? Do we want lawyers to lead the movement? And most of us gagged at the thought. So we said: at the very least we ought to organize the capacity to survive the onslaught — and that means the ability to go underground, to have false ID, to travel, to act with some freedom in the face of repression. And that we did; we began that in the fall of 1969.   *Bill*

I thought about the consequences of becoming a political defendant. I'd organized law students to work on legal defense for several years and I was close enough to the Chicago 8 conspiracy trial to be aware of how much time, energy, and resources went into that strategy and other similar legal strategies around the country. So I was very conscious that, on the one hand, it could be a brilliant forum in which to argue ideas about the validity, the legality, the morality, the ethical substance of the war and injustice. On the other hand, it did divert people away from being organizers into defending themselves as well as the ideas. And that's the dilemma of it. You don't want to be in a defensive posture; sometimes history puts you there but you really don't want that as your main strategy. You mainly want to be organizers.

Bernardine

In February 1970, the elected officers of SDS, all Weathermen, simply closed down the SDS National Office.

Somebody called the University of Wisconsin archivist and they took all the stuff out so all the materials landed in a library as we found ourselves descending and going underground.   *Bill*

They figured that there was no longer any space for an open mass-based organization.   *Carl O*

They closed up the National Office. All over the country there were SDS chapters that were functioning — there was this or that fight within them, they had this or that craziness — but it was a functioning, on-the-ground organization. What they did was they cut its head off.   *Bob*

We made tremendous mistakes in 1969 in allowing SDS to break apart and not fighting to preserve it more. I think our understanding of how to escalate to the next level of militancy was erratic and ill-informed in many ways.   *Cathy*

We underestimated — and this is obvious with retrospect but it was even obvious to us a year later — how important it was to continue the movement in its open, campus-based, high school-based, community-based form.   *Bernardine*

It seemed to me then and, on balance, it still seems to me now, that regardless of government actions against us we had to keep an open organization going. If we started pulling into ourselves, if we started copying the crimes of the state, so to speak, then we would necessarily lose touch with our base, become ingrown and self-absorbed, lost in passwords and safe houses. And you could say that would be the end of the organized protest movement.   *Carl O*

They killed the movement before its natural death. We could ask ourselves how long would SDS have survived. I actually don't think it would have survived too much longer but that's just a guess.   *Bob*

I thought that for SDS to destroy itself at the moment of its greatest contribution and potential power was just so crazy as to be the work, somehow, of the devil.   *Carl O*

There was an intensifying feeling that we were not going to survive the next few months and an intensifying feeling of repression and struggle. And there was a lot of struggle internally about the direction we ought to take. And there was some discussion about wanting the organization to go on, that we weren't going to go underground as an organization — but the townhouse trumped all that.   *Bill*

TOWNHOUSE

In March 1970, an accidental explosion destroyed a townhouse in New York's Greenwich Village, that was owned by Cathy Wilkerson's father. The explosion killed three Weathermen: Ted Gold, Diana Oughton, and Terry Robbins.

A group of friends, dear friends, and colleagues blew themselves up — created an explosion that blew themselves up — in the process of trying to make bombs that were extremely powerful and dangerous. That was a devastating moment of realization. The loss of people that we knew, the death, the sense of no turning back, of having crossed a river — were too hard to absorb, overwhelming in their implications.   *Bernardine*

And we scattered, without a lot of concern for what else would happen.
                                                                          Bill

So that a whole group of us who had talked about creating a clandestine apparatus all disappeared on hearing of the townhouse. And it forced us also back into ourselves and forced us into a re-assessment of what happened and why — and what path we were going to take.   *Bernardine*

The townhouse has become a calendar date — and in some ways marks the end of SDS.   *Cathy*

It was something, I think, that shocked and appalled the vast majority of people in SDS.   *Carolyn*

Let's not make any mistake about this, OK — 97, 98, 99% of the anti-war activists, for that matter of SDS activists in particular, wanted no part of a Weatherman scenario. People had arguments about whether the violent turn was a good thing or not, and some shared the romance — at a safe remove — but very few people joined the Weather Underground. I don't think there were ever more than a couple hundred.   *Todd*

And yet, one of the things that bothers me is that it's a part of our legacy. For whether I like it or not, they were a part of us. They came out of us. I'll never understand how they made that transition — how they went from democratic, peace-loving people to building bombs. But they did.   *Carolyn*

I knew everybody in the townhouse. They were all people I had lived with, worked with. Some of them were people I cared deeply about. So it was a personal tragedy. It was searing — that my comrades had done this horrific thing.   *Jane*

How is it that people I knew so well, people I loved, suddenly were strangers to me, had politics I couldn't even imagine where they were coming from? I hated the war, I hated racism — and they can't possibly argue that they hated it more than I did. That's impossible. A big part of me will never forgive them. I think they destroyed the movement.   *Carolyn*

I did not agree with what they were doing but in some way I felt that they were my agent, despite the fact that I didn't agree with it, because I could fully understand the rage and the despair and the frustration that they felt.
        Jane

I think there were unnecessary casualties — both in terms of human life but far more extensive was the damage to people's emotional lives for years to come, the great many who were hurt and demoralized by the chaos of 1969-70. I think we did enormous damage to ourselves.   *Cathy*

The thing the townhouse symbolized is that we all have within us the potential to do really, really evil, profoundly wrong things; to act in profoundly wrong ways, things that are just immoral. People you otherwise know to have tremendous potential for good can somehow turn a corner and go down a path that is, to use religious terms, evil. And that power is within all of us — and it's an act of grace when you don't turn that corner.   *Jane*

I personally always felt that I was so grounded in communities that a lot of what they were talking about made no sense to me — and even if it made sense to me intellectually, I didn't see what the point of it was. So as SDS imploded, I always felt very thankful and fortunate — I felt that I had maintained my sense of balance because I had maintained my connections to people in communities. Unless it made sense to me in terms of the people in the community, it didn't make much sense to me.   *Carol*

NEW MORNING

The townhouse made us re-assess where we were going, who we were, and where we fit in with the broad anti-war movement. The timing of figuring that out amongst ourselves coincided with the escalation of the war into Cambodia and Laos, the bombing of Cambodia, the attack on students at Jackson State and Kent State and the murdering of American campus students — and a re-flowering of a campus-based and mass student-based opposition to the war.   *Bernardine*

They suddenly realized what they were doing — it did sort of shock them into a reality.   *Jane*

We ended up rejecting a military strategy, ended up rejecting a strategy that would involve loss of life, ended up rejecting a strategy of hurting innocent civilians. We ended up with the notion that our job as an underground was to be a voice, a prod, a critic, an example of the vulnerability and the powerlessness of the government — that we'd conduct symbolic actions but that they'd be symbolic and not pretend to be of a military nature, and we'd organize ourselves to not be involved in the loss of life — our own or anyone else's.

We spent most of 1970 creating an underground that wouldn't get caught, learning how to be clandestine and stay in touch with each other and stay in touch with people who were not underground. We also discussed the implications of the townhouse — and who we were and what we wanted to be.

Bernardine

Bernardine Dohrn, 1968

We wanted to communicate to a lot of people like ourselves but who we were not in touch with directly, the lessons from the townhouse. And we felt responsible to try to have that discussion go out in a much broader and public way — to not have people kill themselves or kill innocent people or harm themselves — and also to be strategic about the use of armed propaganda and militant action generally and to recognize the need for popular organizing and popular struggle. We thought it important to give up the sectarian insanity that we'd all gotten ensnared in: that there was a single right thing to do at any given moment — and if only we could figure out what it was, all would be well in the world and we'd be reborn into a cooperative, peaceful era. So that notion that there were multiple forms of activity that were appropriate and they could coexist — you didn't have to be perfect about everything — we felt was a lesson that we learned at a terrible cost.

New Morning – Changing Weather was a statement we issued from underground nine months after the townhouse explosion.

Bernardine

It has been nine months since the townhouse explosion. In that time the future of our revolution has been changed decisively. A growing illegal organization of young women and men can live and fight and love inside Babylon. The FBI can't catch us; we've pierced their bullet-proof shield. But the townhouse forever destroyed our belief that armed struggle is the only real revolutionary struggle.

It is time for the movement to go out into the air, to organize, to risk calling rallies and demonstrations, to convince that mass actions against the war and in support of rebellions do make a difference . . . The deaths of three friends ended our military conception of what were are doing. . . . it was clear that more had been wrong with our direction than technical inexperience.

New Morning — Changing Weather, November 1970

So far as I know, the only people they ever blew up was themselves, in the townhouse explosion.   *Carl O*

Whatever they did, and I don't want to make excuses for them, we've got to remember that the whole Weatherman episode didn't equal the napalming of one Vietnamese village — in its intensity or in its mistakenness — and keep our eyes on who the main criminals were.   *Steve*

16
The War Is Over

When President Nixon invaded Cambodia in the spring of 1970, demonstrations began happening across the country and at Kent State the National Guard shot into a group of demonstrators. And then the whole country came unglued. *Robert*

Four students were killed by the National Guard at Kent State University in Ohio and ten days later two students were killed by police at Jackson State College in Mississippi.

KENT STATE
UNIVERSITY
MAY 4th, 1970

There were demonstrations at over 1000 schools. Students at 500 campuses went on strike and some closed down for the rest of the school year. Although SDS no longer existed as a national organization, some chapters still existed while others had simply changed their name and continued. Many who had been active in SDS remained active after its collapse.

Austin, Texas, May 1970

We had a demonstration in 1970 with 25,000 people in it. The demonstration went from the University of Texas downtown, then back up another street past the state Capitol to the university. In 1963, in the fall, there were three demonstrators, and in 1970 in the spring there were 25,000 demonstrators — that was probably the largest demonstration in Austin.   *Robert*

I remember walking in this procession where there were clergy and faculty and students and the general population. And someone I had been in school with in 1967 saw me there and said, "You must feel like a mother to this." But truly, it was so amazing to see that grow, to see that many people, and know that it had started from such a small group of committed individuals.   *Alice*

Alice Embree at demonstration, Austin, May 1970

The biggest demonstrations in American history were carried on by students after Kent State. Millions of people participated in those over a period of weeks. SDS was gone by then. This was a bottom-up, grass-roots rolling movement of students, and faculty in many cases. I found that probably the most inspiring single moment in the whole decade in terms of grass roots initiative.   *Dick*

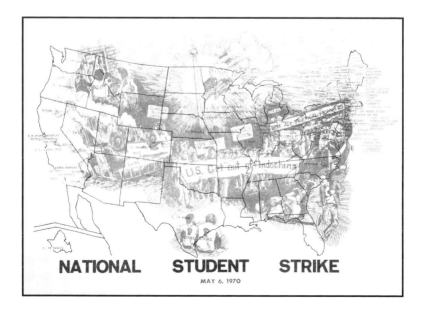

NATIONAL   STUDENT   STRIKE
MAY 6, 1970

It's very symbolic that Kent State happened after the townhouse, after this major student organization had imploded on itself. Then one of the most memorable student struggles happened, because of all of the dynamic that had been set up so effectively that it could continue — and did continue — for several years without any national structure whatsoever.   *Cathy*

It seemed to me we had fulfilled something that we had planned from the beginning if so many people could take creative action so well all across the country without leadership. Well, they had their own leadership.   *Dick*

The plowing of the ground that SDS had been doing for a decade did lead to another generation of activists. A lot of new students, younger students, who had not been part of the Sixties history, now we're in 1970 and they're part of the '70s history — re-learning again how to communicate, how to turn out leaflets, how to deal with people being arrested, how to coordinate with other campuses, how to formulate their demands, how to stay international and to stay local. All of those lessons, of course, can only be learned through the doing. And it was happening again.   *Bernardine*

The war did not end then. There were pullbacks but the war dragged on for five more years. Finally, on April 30, 1975, the Vietnamese National Liberation Front and the North Vietnamese armies entered Saigon. The US abandoned its embassy — and the war was finally over.

APRIL 30, 1975

To me the '60s begins February 1, 1960 with the sit-in of black students at a lunch counter in Greensboro — and ends April 30, 1975. I know that's five years in addition but that's really the '60s.

It ends with those indelible images of the United States running out of Vietnam, dangling onto helicopters, shredding documents at the embassy, leaving behind B-52s costing hundreds of billions of dollars apiece and gadgetry and the utter failure of the technological imposition of domination and might. There was not even a retreat, generals getting together, shaking hands, discussing the terms of the surrender, nothing like that.

It was chaos, it was a rout, it was the total and utter humiliation and defeat of US strategy.   *Bernardine*

The end of the war was this mad scramble out — just turning tail and fleeing, in a totally self-serving way. And humiliating, it was truly humiliating, abandoning the Vietnamese who we had been fighting for, just turning tail and fleeing.

Jane

I flipped on the radio in the morning and there was news that Saigon was falling, or was going to fall imminently. And I sat there transfixed. And I listened and I listened, I just sat there in this reverie thinking: my gosh, this is actually happening, this is coming to an end. These people are going to be left alone.

Folks who I had not seen or talked to in a year or two were calling that night. There was a bit of a transcontinental reunion; we were sharing memories. It was the culmination of a generation's worth of effort.

Mark

I cried. I was so happy. For me the war ended when the helicopter carried out the last guy. And I just remember tears of joy. I watched it on TV. I felt like a heavy weight had been lifted, that this period had come to an end.

Carl D

Poster made by singer Phil Ochs, 1975

That night we had a celebration at the big Unitarian church in downtown Los Angeles. Everybody's kissing and hugging and celebrating and cheering and singing. For my oldest daughter, ever since she was born — by this time she was six years old — the war had been a permanent feature of her life, her entire early childhood. She had been carried in backpacks and in strollers to demonstration after demonstration. And I remember her being up on the stage with us at this rally and saying, "What are we going to do now?"   *Sue*

I went to a conference in Washington [late 1974] where I. F. Stone spoke and he said the next Vietnam is the Middle East. And he gave a very compelling speech and said that it was going to be a conflict that was going to embroil the United States and had deep moral issues and was going to be more divisive even than Vietnam. And he was right.   *Vivian*

17
Legacy

The Sixties changed us in very profound and lasting ways — and they changed America.

Those who think that SDS ended in 1969 are wrong. SDS as an organization fell apart.   *Dick*

SDS, as far as I see, never stopped because I never considered it as the organizational entity. It fused with the movement and the movement is wider and broader than it ever was.   *Alan*

The legacy is the organizational skills that we gained — the feeling of what it means to work as a group of people committed to change and realizing some of that. What does it take to make change? How do you make change? How do you do the work on a day-to-day basis? How do you live that kind of life? That for me is the legacy.   *Judy*

Whenever you have an organization that is as rich and deep and powerful as SDS, the legacy of that organization will continue and the people that came out of it are going to continue to do what they do on and on.   *Cathy*

I'm still here. I'm still basically in the same area and in the same business — of politics, with a small 'p'.   *Junius*

I kept going, we all kept going, and we are all still going.   *Casey*

The media has delighted in picking out the occasional person who became a stockbroker or an insurance dealer and tried to portray those people as typical of a whole generation. But it's not the case. People have remained remarkably constant.   *Steve*

We're everywhere. Every institution in American life has a core of us somewhere — people out there trying to make their values explicit.   *Carl D*

My values are the same — I'm working in a different way. A lot of what I can do now, as an organizer of my own school, is from my experience within SDS more than thirty years ago. It's had that long-term influence on me — and then indirectly on the people I work with and the children that we serve.   *Judy*

A surprisingly large number of that generation went and found ways to have jobs and make incomes that were consistent with what they had believed all along. People went into teaching or social work or health care or the arts or environmental law and advocacy. People found ways of carrying on what they'd been doing — but within the regular workday world.   *Steve*

That whole period of time — of activism, of principles, of values, of valuing people, valuing life — I think had a profound effect on our country and certainly on the rest of our generation and the generations to follow.   *Carol*

There are things we take for granted now in this country that were never even dreamt of when we were fighting for them in the Sixties.   *Mark*

How much of it you can exactly attribute to SDS, and how much you can exactly attribute to SNCC, and how much exactly to the anti-war movement — it's impossible to set up those compartments. But you can look at the entire picture.   *Steve*

Race relations will never be the same. I mean, white supremacy will never be common sense again. Women, the same thing — the same shift has happened with women.   *Jane*

Nobody really knew then how really important the women's movement would become. I mean, it's totally changed America. It's changed the generations behind us.   *Marilyn*

I remember growing up and there were so few things that women could really do. And my daughter now can look at the world and choose from all manner of occupations. Those changes were fought — they were fought and won.   *Alice*

When I left the movement, I went into television news. Let me tell you, there were virtually no women, much less black women, in television news. But one of the things SDS had done for me — and my parents had laid the groundwork, let me not dismiss them — but one of the things that happened to me coming out of the movement was there was nothing I couldn't do. Anything I wanted to do, I could do. I was not going to be stopped because I was a female, I was not going to be stopped because I was black. When we started off, that wasn't true; there were a whole bunch of things I couldn't do, there were whole worlds that were closed to me. The movement changed me and I think I helped change the world.   *Carolyn*

We played a vital role in forging the movement against the Vietnam War — and that's the most important thing we did.   *Sue*

I think we were the conscience of America. I think in some ways we saved the soul of America by protesting the war in Vietnam.   *Jeff*

This country did produce an important segment of a few generations that really did believe in the great ideas of American democracy — and were willing to put their lives on the line to put those values into practice.

Carl O

I'm glad I did what I did, small as it was, trying to end this horrendous war in Vietnam.   *Todd*

I'm a father now. I have an answer to the question, "What did you do during the war?" And it's an answer I'm really proud of.   *Bob*

The notion that any US military intervention could turn into a Vietnam does remain a legacy and does put a break on US aggression. The belief in American military and technological invincibility was shattered.

Bernardine

We drove a spike through the heart of a conscripted army. It will be decades before the people who run this country will simply be able to dragoon people into the military.   *Mark*

I think we also stopped a number of wars, potential wars. We said one of the goals was not to stop just Vietnam but to stop the seventh Vietnam. We changed foreign policy in significant ways.   *Jane*

In a certain sense we are all veterans of the Vietnam War. Those who fought there died or were wounded or were horrified. But those of us who opposed it on the home front had an experience that will never leave us — in good ways and bad ways. We felt extreme urgency and often felt inadequate to the task. People did things, took actions, that determined the rest of their lives. Something that molds your life is something of which you are a veteran.   *Bob*

I had a small part to play in helping to change the world — I have no regrets. That doesn't mean there aren't things I wouldn't do differently — there are plenty of those. I made lots of mistakes and I accept responsibility for all of them. But regrets? No, I don't have any regrets.   *Carl D*

Even when it looks like young people are apathetic and they're just self-involved — and certainly it's different than it was for us — they start so much ahead of where we were. They start with understandings that are beyond where we started. I think we gave them that.   *Carol*

There are probably more people involved in organizing work right now than ever were involved in the Sixties. There are little community organizations all around, single-issue things, everywhere.   *Robert*

The generations looking back could look at what we did and say, "Gee, those people put everything they had into it and yet problems still exist, racism is still here, they didn't 'win.'" Well, that's also a short-sighted view of what winning means. Winning is about taking another step toward, down the line, achieving a better society, a better life for our children and for the next generations — and we took a step in that direction.   *Mike*

We tried to change the culture of this country — that students are not meant to be passive recipients or vessels of knowledge but can actually play a role in not only making change but leading change. And that you can learn from students, not just from teachers. The university has never been, and will never be, the same.   *Sue*

We still face an environmental catastrophe, but if environmental catastrophe is to be averted, it's an outcome of the '60s.   *Jane*

We made the word democracy a real word. When we talked about people making the decisions that affect their own lives, we meant it.   *Carolyn*

That democracy that we fought for is not enough. You can have a manipulated democracy. You can have a democracy in which people go through the motions of participating and voting but they don't know what they're talking about because they don't have information, because the media is more and more consolidated, it follows a kind of corporate slant, or you could be even more cynical and say you get more and more entertainment instead of information.

So I think we have to go beyond the discussion of democracy back to the other elements of Port Huron, which is the problems of greed and too much concentration of wealth and the need for healing racial divisions by public action.   *Tom*

This society has so many means of diverting people from thinking, and entertaining them, that unless you can devise bold activities that break through that, you're never going to be heard and you're never going to be listened to.   *Juan*

The big legacy is a very mixed one — that shattering of the belief that American democracy and leaders are to be trusted. I thought that was entirely an asset until the last ten years. I have come to believe that the cynicism about civic life and political life and democratic public life is itself corrosive and destructive.   *Bernardine*

We got the right to vote in the South 'cause we stuck together. We organized. You can't get anything unless you organize.   *Junius*

People think we knew what we were doing, that we knew we were making history, that we were so clever and so sophisticated. And I think we need to let people know that we didn't know what we were doing, we had no idea we would make history, and we only did things because we thought they were right.   *Vivian*

We were value-based — and that is really, really important.   *Sharon*

The feeling the world could be a better place, that was really what it was.

Elizabeth

I still look back on it and think the dream was not wrong and the dream was worth dreaming.   *Bill*

One of the things that is a lesson that will last forever is that a small group of people can make a difference — and you really can change events. Politicians will just go whatever way the wind blows. Well, we were the people making the wind blow!   *Alice*

Interviewees

Jane Adams. Raised in southern Illinois, Jane attended Antioch College and Southern Illinois University before dropping out to work first in the civil rights movement in Mississippi and then in the growing anti-war movement. She worked for SDS as a regional traveler around the Midwest, then as national secretary in 1966, and later in Cleveland and Oklahoma. She is now a professor of anthropology at Southern Illinois University and the author of several books.

Bill Ayers. Bill was raised in Chicago, went to the University of Michigan, and joined SDS as the war in Vietnam heated up. He taught for several years in a progressive alternative school in Ann Arbor but turned his energy full time to stopping the war in 1968 and became a regional organizer for SDS and then internal education secretary in 1969. He was a founder of Weatherman. He is now a professor of education at the University of Illinois at Chicago and author of several books on education. He is co-author of *Sing a Battle Song* and his memoir of the '60s is titled *Fugitive Days*.

Carolyn Craven. Carolyn grew up in Chicago and became involved in the civil rights movement and SDS while at Goucher College. In 1964, she dropped out of college and worked in the SDS National Office. In 1965 she moved to San Francisco and helped set up SDS's first regional office. She later became a radio and television journalist in San Francisco and also was White House correspondent for NPR and co-host of South Africa Now. Carolyn died in November 2000.

Carl Davidson. Carl grew up in Aliquippa, in western Pennsylvania, attended Penn State University, where he became involved with SDS, and then graduate school in philosophy at the University of Nebraska. He dropped out of school after participating in the civil right march through Mississippi in 1966 and then went to work in the SDS National Office. He was elected vice-president in 1966 and then inter-organizational secretary in 1967. He currently teaches computer repair to inner-city kids and prisoners in Chicago. While now emphasizing new theoretical work, he never stopped his activism for peace and human rights.

Bernardine Dohrn. Bernardine grew up in Chicago and Milwaukee, became involved with the civil rights movement in the mid-1960s while in law school at the University of Chicago. She joined SDS as the war and anti-draft movement heated up and organized National Lawyers Guild student chapters. In 1968 she was elected national inter-organizational secretary of SDS. She later joined Weatherman. She is now the director of the Children and Family Justice Center of the Northwestern University School of Law. She is co-author of *Sing a Battle Song*.

Alice Embree. Alice grew up in Austin and was one of the early SDS members at the University of Texas. In the late Sixties she did research for the North American Committee on Latin America (NACLA) and also worked with the *RAT* newspaper in New York. She still lives in Austin and is active in anti-war, union, and women's issues.

Dick Flacks. Dick grew up in New York, joined SDS in 1962 while at the University of Michigan, and continued SDS and anti-war activities when he began teaching at the University of Chicago in 1964. He recently retired as professor of sociology at UC Santa Barbara. He and his wife Mickey have been community activists in Santa Barbara for nearly forty years.

Todd Gitlin. Todd grew up in New York, became involved in the peace movement while at Harvard in the early 1960s, joined SDS in 1962, and served as president in 1963–64. While in graduate school at the University of Michigan, he was coordinator of SDS's Peace Research and Action Project. He later worked with SDS's Chicago ERAP project and co-wrote *Uptown: Poor Whites in Chicago* about the people there. He taught sociology at UC Berkeley, media studies at New York University, and is now a professor of journalism and sociology at Columbia University. He is the author of many books, including *The Sixties: Years of Hope, Days of Rage*.

Carol Glassman. Carol grew up in Brooklyn, NY, and learned about SDS while at Smith College. After graduation in 1964, she worked as a community organizer in SDS's Newark ERAP project where she remained until 1968. Then, along with other SDSers, she moved to the Ironbound neighborhood of Newark and began another organizing project. She left in 1978 to return to school. She now teaches social work and has a private psychotherapy practice in New York.

Juan Gonzalez. Juan was born in Puerto Rico and grew up in East Harlem and Brooklyn, NY. He joined SDS while at Columbia University. He was a founder and leader of the Young Lords Party. A journalist for nearly 30 years, he has been a staff columnist for the NY *Daily News* since 1987, a co-host of Pacifica's *Democracy Now* since 1996, and a founder and past president of the National Association of Hispanic Journalists. He is the author of several books, including *Harvest of Empire: A History of Chicanos in America* and *Fallout: The Environmental Consequences of the World Trade Center Collapse*.

Alan Haber. Alan grew up primarily in Ann Arbor, Michigan, with a few years in Washington, DC, and a year in post-war Germany. He entered the University of Michigan in 1954 planning to be a chemist. In 1959 he was hired to be the field secretary for a small and fairly inactive student organization that had recently changed its name to SDS and he soon convinced the group to embrace his vision for a broader and more active student organization. He served as SDS's first president from 1960-62. He is now a cabinet-maker in Ann Arbor, Michigan, and remains a political organizer. He is currently helping in the creation of a new SDS.

Casey Hayden. Casey (born Sandra Cason) grew up in segregated east Texas and became involved in the civil rights movement while at the University of Texas in the late 1950s. She was a founding member of SDS and SNCC. She worked for SNCC (Student Nonviolent Coordinating Committee) until 'black power' led her to leave the South and she organized white women in SDS's Chicago ERAP project. In 1965 she co-authored a short paper titled *"Sex and Caste"* which helped set off the women's movement within SDS and beyond. She currently lives in Tucson and is a contributor to *Deep in our Hearts: Nine White Women in the Freedom Movement*.

Tom Hayden. Tom grew up attending Catholic schools in Royal Oak, Michigan, and became involved in SDS when he was editor of the student paper at the University of Michigan. He moved to Atlanta where he reported on the southern civil rights movement for SDS. He was elected president of SDS in 1962 and in 1964 went to work in the Newark ERAP project where he remained until 1967. For years after that he devoted himself full time to organizing against the war in Vietnam. He helped organize anti-war protests at the Democratic convention in August 1968 and was indicted for conspiring to incite violence there. Although he was ultimately acquitted on appeal, he spent much of the next few years in court and jail. By that time he had moved to California where he continued to be an activist, writer, and later California State Senator from Los Angeles. He now teaches at the Claremont Colleges and is the author of numerous books, including *Reunion: A Memoir.*

Mark Kleiman. Mark was a high school member of SDS in Los Angeles when he was kicked out of school for distributing an SDS anti-war leaflet. He then worked full time for civil rights and against the war in Los Angeles and later in Chicago in the National Office and as northern California regional organizer in San Francisco. He is currently a lawyer in Los Angeles, specializing in defending whistle-blowers.

Sue Eanet Klonsky. Sue grew up in Washington DC and discovered SDS and the anti-war movement while at Ithaca College in 1965. As the war escalated, she became active in the Cornell SDS chapter, dropped out of school to work against the Vietnam war, headed the NY SDS regional office in 1965, and later worked in the Los Angeles regional office and the National Office in Chicago. She now works for school reform in Chicago.

Sharon Jeffrey Lehrer. Sharon grew up in Detroit and was one of the first members of SDS in 1960 at the University of Michigan. After graduation in 1963, she worked full time in the civil rights movement, primarily with the Northern Student Movement, and later in SDS's Cleveland ERAP project. She is currently a leadership coach and co-owner of an art gallery north of San Francisco.

Steve Max. Steve became a political organizer for reform Democratic candidates fresh out of high school in New York in the early 1960s, joined SDS in 1962, was an early SDS field secretary, and later director of its Political Education Project. He still lives in New York and since 1973 he has been the associate director of the Midwest Academy, a Chicago-based training and consulting center for progressive organizing.

Carl Oglesby. Carl grew up in Akron, Ohio, attended Kent State University and was a budding playwright. In 1965 he was working in Ann Arbor, Michigan, as a writer for a defense contractor, finishing college at the University of Michigan, and was married with three kids when he began to learn about Vietnam and was horrified by what he learned. SDS members found him and in quick succession he joined SDS, spoke at the first teach-in at Ann Arbor, quit his job, was elected president of SDS in 1965, became one of SDS's best-known speakers, and began years of traveling around the country speaking against the war. He now lives in western Massachusetts and is the author of several books, including a forthcoming memoir of the Sixties.

Robert Pardun. Robert was born in Kansas, grew up in Pueblo, Colorado, and was one of the founders of the SDS chapter at the University of Texas in 1963, where he was a graduate student in mathematics. He dropped out of school to become a regional traveler for SDS and was elected internal education secretary in 1967. He later lived on a commune in the Ozark Mountains and then became a metal worker. He returned to school, obtained his MA, and became a math instructor in the mid 1990s. He now lives in the Santa Cruz mountains of California and is the author of *Prairie Radical: A Journey through the Sixties.*

Bob Ross. Bob grew up in the Bronx, NY, near Yankee Stadium, and was one of the first people to join SDS at the University of Michigan in 1960. He was vice-president of SDS in 1961–62. When he went to the University of Chicago for graduate school in 1964, he helped start the SDS chapter there and also worked in SDS's Chicago ERAP project. He is now a professor of sociology at Clark University in Worcester, Massachusetts, and an anti-sweatshop campaigner. He is the author of *Slaves to Fashion: Poverty and Abuse in the New Sweatshops.*

Vivian Leburg Rothstein. Vivian grew up largely in Los Angeles, was at UC Berkeley during the Free Speech Movement, went to Mississippi to work with the civil rights movement, then joined SDS's Chicago ERAP project to continue organizing in the North. She later became very active in the women's movement. For many years, she served as director of a homeless services organization and is currently deputy director of the Los Angeles

Alliance for a New Economy where she works on living-wage legislation to address low-wage poverty.

Judy Schiffer Perez. Judy was born in New York and grew up in Pennsylvania and then Port Arthur, Texas. She was one of the early members of SDS at the University of Texas. She later moved to Los Angeles where she helped start the SDS regional office there. She has spent many years teaching in Los Angeles inner-city schools, and is now principal of an elementary school and is on the executive board of her union.

Jeff Shero Nightbyrd. Jeff grew up in Texas and moved with his family to various Air Force bases. He was one of the first members of SDS at the University of Texas and was active in the southern civil rights movement. He helped found *The Rag* in Austin later the New York *RAT: Subterranean News*. He was elected vice-president of SDS in 1965, and edited SDS's *New Left Notes*. He has been active in civil liberties questions. He currently lives in Austin, Texas, and Louisiana, works in the movie industry, and owns Acclaim Talent.

Mike Spiegel. Mike grew up in Portland, Oregon and joined SDS while at Harvard in the mid 1960s. He was elected national secretary in 1967 and dropped out of school to devote his time to anti-war organizing. He is currently a lawyer in New York, specializing in police brutality and death penalty cases.

Elizabeth Stanley. Elizabeth grew up in Los Angeles, joined SDS while a freshman at Harvard in 1968, and soon dropped out of college to work against the war. She has worked with various labor unions and is now a film producer in Los Angeles.

Marilyn Salzman Webb. Marilyn was born in Brooklyn, NY, and grew up on Long Island. She joined SDS in Chicago and was active in both SDS and the women's movement in Chicago and Washington, DC. She continued to be active in the women's movement, founding the women's paper, *Off Our Backs*, and the Women's Studies Department at Goddard College, the first women's studies program in the country. She currently lives half the year in New York where she is a writer and journalist and an advocate for better care for the dying and the other half in Illinois where she is co-chair of the journalism program at Knox College. She is the author of *The Good Death: The New American Search to Reshape the End of Life*.

Cathy Wilkerson. Cathy grew up in Connecticut and became involved in the civil rights movement and SDS in 1963 while at Swarthmore College. She later worked in the SDS National Office and edited SDS's newspaper, *New Left Notes*. In 1968, she moved to Washington DC to begin an SDS regional office there. She later joined Weatherman. She currently teaches math to inner-city kids and teachers in New York. Her forthcoming memoir will be out in the fall of 2007.

Junius Williams. Junius was raised in Richmond, Virginia, went to Amherst College, and worked in the civil rights movement with SNCC. He worked with SDS's Newark ERAP project during summer vacations and in his spare time while continuing at Yale Law School. He has been in Newark ever since, serving as campaign manager for Ken Gibson, Newark's first black mayor, and director of the Model Cities program. He currently directs the Abbott Leadership Institute at Rutgers University Newark and has evolved as an advocate, bluesman, and griot.

Helen Garvy. Helen was born in New York and became active in the civil rights, university reform, and peace movements while in college at Harvard in the early sixties. She helped start the Harvard SDS chapter in 1963 and was elected assistant national secretary of SDS in 1964 and spent the next year in the National Office where she also edited the *SDS Bulletin*. She worked in SDS's ERAP project in Hoboken, New Jersey, and in 1967 moved to San Francisco to teach in an alternative school, while continuing her involvement in SDS and anti-war activities.

Helen has been making films for 20 years as a producer, director, writer, and/or editor. She is also a writer and the author of several books. She now lives in the Santa Cruz mountains of California and continues to be a political activist. This book is adapted from her film, *Rebels with a Cause*.

SDS convention, 1965

SDS Organizational Structure

The core of SDS was its local chapters, primarily on college campuses but also in high schools. Chapters had autonomy and decided how they would organize themselves and what issues they would focus on and how. The role of the National Office was generally to help chapters and disseminate information, which included the SDS paper, originally the *SDS Bulletin* which in 1965 became *New Left Notes*, as well as pamphlets on a variety of issues. As SDS grew, the national organization sometimes proposed programs but participation, and how to participate, was always up to the chapters.

General national policy decisions were made at the SDS annual summer conventions, where every SDS member attending had a vote. The conventions elected officers, which were for one year terms. By tradition, people served only one term. Convention decisions were supplemented by decisions made by quarterly national council meetings, composed of representatives from each chapter as well as some elected at-large members.

From 1960 until mid-1967 the main SDS officers were the president and vice president. The national secretary and assistant national secretary ran day-to-day operations in the National Office, assisted by other staff as size and needs dictated. There were also sometimes campus travelers who would visit existing chapters and help organize new ones. Other jobs and titles were created as needs arose.

The 1967 SDS convention decided to have the primary officers be based full time in the National Office, although they would also travel to chapters, and changed the titles to more closely reflect the work they did. The new officers were: national secretary, inter-organizational secretary, and education secretary.

The SDS National Office was in New York until May, 1965, and in Chicago after that. As SDS grew, regional offices were started, either with the encouragement of the National Office or by chapters in the regions. Many had full-time staffs. Staffs in national and regional offices were usually a combination of people paid subsistence wages and volunteers.

Acknowledgements

There are so very many people who have helped in a variety of ways with both the film and the book, far too many to mention them all. I, of course, want to especially thank those whose interviews are included in the book — but also many, many others who talked with me about their experiences; who contributed ideas; who found old photos, posters, buttons for me to include; who allowed me to use their photos; and who gave me much useful feedback on the film in progress and the book. I especially want to thank a few who helped in preparing the book: Susan Boiko, Lincoln Cushing, Becca Gourevitch, Meg Holmberg, Sue Klonsky, Dickie Magidoff, Brigid McCaw, Witt Monts, Michael Rossman. And Robert Pardun!

PHOTO AND POSTER CREDITS

Austin History Center, Austin Public Library (A566-55-685) 79

Jude Binder 122

Jay Cantor 158r

Center for the Study of Political Graphics archive 131r, 196

Frank Cieciorka 208

Tom Copi 11, 59, 63, 231

Howie Epstein 13, 31, 33b, 36b & r, 39, 40, 138, 139, 140m & b, 141, 142, 151b, 161, 163, 165, 167

Economic Research and Action Project 32b, 33t, 34r, 35, 36t & l

David Fenton/Liberation News Service 211

Helen Garvy 71, 110

Todd Gitlin 9, 20, 34t

D. Gorton 102

Harvey Hacker 158l

Nancy Hollander 34t & b, 37

Robert Joyce Photograph Collection, Courtesy of Historical Collections and Labor Archives, Special Collections Library, The Pennsylvania State University: front cover, 28, 46, 47, 48, 49, 70

C. Clark Kissinger 34m, 45, 53, 72

Liberation News Service 151t

Bob Machover and Norm Fruchter, From *Troublemakers* 32t

Mississippi Department of Archives and History: Newsfilm Collection 25

Jeff Shero Nightbyrd 18, 19, 50, 54, 66b, 73, 74, 84, 113, 153

Robert Pardun archives 17, 51, 65, 66t, 175, 177–78, 182–86

Roz Payne, Newsreel Archive 140t, 144, 155

Bill Phillips 15t

Alan Pogue 234, 235t

I.C. Rapoport 41

Walter P Reuther Library, Wayne State University 10, 15

Harvey Richards. From *Critical Focus, The Black and White Photographs of Harvey Wilson Richards* by Paul Richards, Estuary Press 123. From Harvey Richards Film Collection, Estuary Press 135, 136, 147

Michael Rossman/ "All of Us or None" Archive. (digital imaging by Lincoln Cushing/ Docs Populi) 58, 76, 86, 133, 134, 137, 170, 171, 198, 200, 209, 215t, 219, 233, 235b, 237

Andrew Sacks/saxpix.com 80, 85, 109, 225

Dan Shapiro: back cover

Lenny Siegel 93, 125l

Jack A. Smith 69, 149, 202, 210

Wes Wilson 115

Wisconsin Historical Society (X3-52382) 29

All materials not credited are from the collection of the author or courtesy of interviewees.

Index

(for index of interviewees, see page 257)

INDEX OF INTERVIEWEES

ORDER FORM

If you can't find REBELS WITH A CAUSE in your local bookstore, it is available directly from Shire Press.

Also available: REBELS WITH A CAUSE, the film, which is available in DVD or VHS formats, and *Prairie Radical* by Robert Pardun

For more information, see www. ShirePressandFilms.com

❖ ❖ ❖

_____ *REBELS WITH A CAUSE* (BOOK) ($18) $ _____

_____ *REBELS WITH A CAUSE* (DVD) ($25)   _____

_____ *REBELS WITH A CAUSE* (VHS) ($25)   _____

_____ *PRAIRIE RADICAL* by Robert Pardun ($15)   _____

shipping total   _____

TOTAL $ _____

(please add $2 shipping for each item)
Please enclose payment with your order.
California residents add sales tax.

❖ ❖ ❖ ❖ ❖ ❖

Send to:

name _____

address _____

_____ zip _____

e-mail (optional) _____

Shire Press ❖ 644 Hester Creek Road, Los Gatos, CA 95033